WOODWORKER'S GUIDE TO
Sharpening

WOODWORKER'S GUIDE TO
Sharpening

JOHN ENGLISH

Fox
Chapel Publishing

1970 Broad Street • East Petersburg, PA 17520
www.FoxChapelPublishing.com

Alan Giagnocavo
President

J. McCrary
Publisher

Peg Couch
Acquisition Editor

John Kelsey
Series Editor

Gretchen Bacon
Editor

Paul M. Hambke
Senior/Managing Editor

Troy Thorne
Creative Direction

Lindsay Hess
Design & Layout

Special thanks to *Woodcraft Magazine* for allowing the reprinting of the plans for John English's sharpening station in the appendix.

ISBN 978-1-56523-309-6

Publisher's Cataloging-in-Publication Data

English, John.

Woodworker's guide to sharpening / John English. -- East Petersburg, PA : Fox Chapel Publishing, c2008.

    p. ; cm.
    ISBN: 978-1-56523-309-6
    Includes index.

    1. Woodworking tools--Sharpening. 2. Sharpening of tools. 3. Knives--Sharpening. 4. Woodwork--Equipment and supplies. I. Title. II. Title: Sharpening.

TT186 .E54 2008
684/.08--dc22   0805

To learn more about the other great books from
Fox Chapel Publishing, or to find a retailer near you,
call toll-free 1-800-457-9112 or visit us at *www.FoxChapelPublishing.com*.

Note to Authors: We are always looking for talented
authors to write new books in our area of woodworking, design,
and related crafts. Please send a brief letter describing your idea to
Peg Couch, Acquisition Editor, 1970 Broad Street, East Petersburg, PA 17520.

Printed in China
10 9 8 7 6 5 4 3 2 1

Dedication

To Dad

Acknowledgments

The author would like to thank all the generous folks who helped compile this book, including, but by no means limited to, David Nittmann and Cindy Drozda; Victoria and David J. Marks; Dave Mathews and James Krenov; Richard Kell, Russ Morash and Norm Abrams of The New Yankee Workshop; Ken Brady at Woodcraft Magazine; Beverly and Sam Maloof and Roslyn Bock at Maloof Woodworking; Peter Taran at VintageSaws.com; Brad Moriarty at JET Tools; Craig Winer at Garrett Wade; Amanda Smith at Plasplugs; Chris Billman; Ross Gobby at Timbecom; Larry Heinonen, Wally Wilson and Ruth Allard at Lee Valley; David Ellsworth; Stephen Feringa at OneWay; David Reed Smith; Brian Burns; Wolfgang Windrich and Serdar Eraslan at Scheppach; Harrelson Stanley at Shapton; Toby Cardew at M-Power Tools; Dr. David Wiltschko; Charlotte Gandy at Crown Hand Tools; Tom Wolz at Carbide Processors; John Kelliher at Rockler; Tara Ward; Mark Owen at Triton; Stephanie Baker at Homier; Stan Watson at DMT; Neil Kennedy, Scott Burke, Russ Cowen at Smith Abrasives; Ray Lanham; Randy Pringle at U.S. Steel; Peter Hewitt at Woodcut Tools; David Long, Tom Peglowski, and Bob Bender at Norton/Saint-Gobain; Melinda Sweet at Grizzly; Les Troyer and Doug Weingart at Hartville Tool; John Rudge; John Michels and Annette Wolf Bensen at General Tool; Jennifer Adams at WMH Tool Group; Helen Duquette at DMT; Ellis Hein; Doug Hicks at August Home/Woodsmith; Don Naples at Lap-Sharp; Dave Medeiros at Specialty Saw; Laurel Cook at Black & Decker/Delta; Brett Evans at AG Russell; John Kelsey and Peg Couch at Fox Chapel; Bill Tarleton; Kevin Neelley; Darrell Feltmate; and my very good friend, Mark Koons.

Contents

Introduction

There is no joy in dullness.

Larry Heinonen, a popular woodshop writer, likens it to sailing with a dropped anchor. The analogy is a good one. The frustration of shearing the edges of a mortise with a dull chisel is akin to that of a sloop dragging an anchor. Both experiences are unnecessary, and both can be dangerous.

I was trained as a cabinetmaker in an era of machines, where hand tools were a dim resource, seldom used, and often abused. Over the decades, my focus has turned to furniture more than casework, and with that change has come a deep appreciation for the skills of past generations. As a writer and reporter, I have been privileged to visit the shops of some of America's finest woodworkers and have always been impressed by their accumulations of ancient and aging hand tools. They are people with vocations. They see no paradox in the joy of labor because, to them, this is not labor. Their dedication to proper sharpening lessens the work and enhances the rewards.

Watching Sam Maloof excavate a mortise with a sharp chisel, during a class at Colorado's Anderson Ranch Arts Center, was one of the inspirations for this book.

The birth of this book

This book was born in summer 2005, high atop the Rockies in central Colorado. I enrolled in a weekend class under the instruction of Sam Maloof, at the Anderson Ranch Arts Center. Maloof was 89-years-old, evincing the energy of a man half his age and the enthusiasm of a teenager. He led a two-day workshop where he used a succession of hand tools to form the parts of one of his inimitable chairs. As I watched him work through the first morning, I kept thinking of ways the job could be done with power tools. Somewhere around mid-afternoon, it finally sunk in. He was having fun! This wasn't a job. I was watching an 89-year-old man work harder than I ever had to shape a piece of wood, and he was having a ball, as you can see above. Sometime that day or the next, he informed us he can't wait to get to the shop every morning, and often works ten hours a day. Indeed, the work is keeping him young.

The key to finding joy in hand tools is keeping them sharp.

Like every woodworker, I had heard the platitude a hundred times. That weekend, it finally registered. Oh, we all pay homage to the sentiment . . . as we reach for a belt sander.

At lunch on the last day, the topic at the table was sharpening. Several of the very experienced woodworkers confessed to finding it confusing. They had developed a small regimen for sharpening in their own shops and, once established, they rarely explored other options. They were furniture builders, not turners or carvers, so their primary needs ran to sharpening chisels and planes. A couple of them confessed to having mismatched panoplies of stones on their benches, many of the stones inherited. They sometimes didn't remember if odd stones were oil or water cleaned, and they often guessed at the grit. But they used them nonetheless, and wouldn't be without them. Dull tools, all agreed, are the province of dull minds. They are accidents waiting to happen.

For me, the result of this weekend was the abiding idea that an organized, simple sharpening process is essential to sound workmanship. There is a great deal of information on sharpening, much of it quite confusing, and choosing the elements of a system can be intimidating. The object of this book is to present those options in a comprehensive fashion, and allow the reader to choose. No specific method is recommended because there is no "right" way of doing things. All have merit.

In this book, I will, however, explain how to sharpen tools in the woodshop and recommend some jobs you may want to leave to a professional. I'll also put some emphasis on completing tasks you can accomplish with a bench stone, the sanding equipment you already own, and/or a dedicated machine, which is usually a slow rotary water stone or a regular bench grinder. Though this book is designed specifically for

woodworkers—it doesn't cover pruning shears or kitchen knives—the same principles can be applied to other tools, and the skills often will transfer.

Whatever choices you make for your sharpening system, the bottom line is woodworking depends on sharp tools and cutters, whether they are paring chisels, router bits, or turning gouges. Sharp tools deliver better results. And sharp tools are safer tools.

It's time to hoist Mr. Heinonen's anchor.

The look on his face shows you that hard work in the shop every day is what keeps the 89-year-old Sam Maloof young and spry.

Photo by Author. Courtesy of Woodcraft Magazine

CHAPTER 1

Safety Overview

Woodworkers sharpen tools so they cut properly. If the sharpening process isn't done correctly, it can cause more problems than it cures. A poor sharpening job can actually blunt an edge. However, when done right, a razor-sharp cutter will slice through wood in a predictable, controlled manner, is far safer to use than a dull one, and is vastly more enjoyable. A sharp tool won't surprise you, and eliminating surprises is the key to safety. So, it's appropriate the journey begins by looking at ways to make sharpening safer.

The dangers of dust

While woodworkers always have been aware of dust hazards, the issue has not been quite as critical in this field as it has been for metalworkers. Perhaps that is because wood particles are larger and less insidious than metal dust. The fact the woodworking industry is confused on the issue hasn't helped either—conflicting data from respected sources is typical. The net result has been that a huge number of woodworkers have adopted a fairly lax attitude toward dust. For example, some will wear a virtually useless comfort (nuisance) mask when operating a belt sander, and many don't even make that effort. One theory is the ill effects are not instantaneous, so people pay them little heed.

When it comes to sharpening, that insipid attitude can be deadly. Sharpening is essentially metalworking, so it requires a shift in the way we think about dust. The visual evidence of sharpening dust is quite strong. For example, **Figure 1-1** shows the residue of metal dust and stone dust left on a piece of white paper placed under a grinder while grinding the primary bevel on a single chisel.

A safety bulletin from the Washington State Department of Labor and Industries maintains that "workers who file saw blades or those who machine tools with tungsten carbide (or other 'hard metal') tips may be exposed to toxic levels of cadmium, a cancer-causing agent, and cobalt, a suspected cancer-causing agent." According to medical studies, the bulletin continues, "Toxic effects of exposure may include kidney disease, asthma, anemia, emphysema, and hard-metal lung disease with reduced lung function."[1]

That is a frightening assertion, and one that applies to professional, full-time metalworkers. Somebody spending just a few days a year sharpening is obviously not exposed to the same degree of hazard. Still, cobalt is a binder for tungsten carbide crystals and can be present in almost every carbide cutter in a woodshop. The U.S. Department of Labor said this about the dangers of grinding carbide tools: "Inhalation of cobalt metal fumes and dust may cause interstitial fibrosis, interstitial pneumonitis, myocardial and thyroid disorders, and sensitization of the respiratory tract and skin. Chronic cobalt poisoning may also produce polycythemia and hyperplasia of the bone marrow."[2]

In layman's terms, that means cobalt fumes and dust may cause unwanted new tissue to grow in the cavities between organs in the human body, and may also contribute to heart, lung, bone, and thyroid problems. Again, the reference is to people employed on a daily basis in metalworking and not to an occasional sharpener. However, there is strong evidence to suggest woodworkers who smoke, perform a lot of sharpening tasks, breathe a lot of wood sanding dust, or are engaged in metalworking as well as woodworking, are at higher risk. Sharpening can be perfectly safe if you take the right precautions, and quite threatening if you ignore them.

Figure 1-1. The residue of metal dust and stone dust from grinding a single chisel indicates the scope of the sharpening dust problem. Inhaling this residue is not wise.

[1] Safety Bulletin 95-1a
[2] http://www.osha.gov/SLTC/healthguidelines/cobaltmetaldustandfume/recognition.html

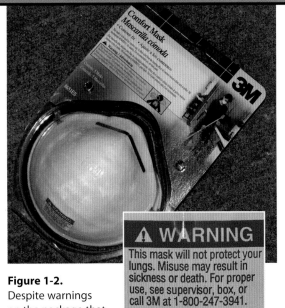

Figure 1-2.
Despite warnings on the package that nuisance masks don't protect lungs, and the obvious lack of fit to the face, people feel a false sense of security and wear them anyway.

> ⚠ **WARNING**
> This mask will not protect your lungs. Misuse may result in sickness or death. For proper use, see supervisor, box, or call 3M at 1-800-247-3941.

The bottom line is grinding and honing produce extremely fine particles that become airborne during sharpening. Many of the particles from the grindstones, the coatings, the binders (the materials that bond the cutter to the blade), and the metals used in the blades themselves, can present a serious health hazard. Inexpensive comfort masks, as shown in **Figure 1-2**, are a problem. They don't seal properly (especially if the wearer has facial hair) and they impart a false sense of security. They can make people feel safe, when in fact they are not. Warnings printed on comfort masks from 3M, Ace Hardware, and other respected suppliers repeatedly tell consumers the masks are not suitable for sanding or sharpening. They are designed to keep large, nonthreatening particles out of the nostrils, and are almost completely ineffective at protecting the lungs.

Sharp or Dull?

Sharpness is a matter of degree. It can be difficult to know when a tool is sharp enough, or too dull, to use safely. A sharp edge slices smoothly through wood fibers rather than tearing them. That means a well-tuned plane or chisel peels a perfect ribbon (see **Figure 1**) or cleaves cleanly through end grain (see **Figure 2**). If the same tool is dull, it may stutter as it travels or become hung up when the grain changes direction. A sharp plane iron sounds sharp—the cutting is continuous and delivers an uninterrupted whoosh as it glides across the wood.

Usually, the sharper a cutter is, the easier it will slice. Sometimes, though, the problem is with the tool rather than the blade. Some tools, such as spokeshaves, can defy the rules every now and then and work better when they are pushed than pulled (see **Figure 3**). Many planes have the iron (blade) set too deeply, which will cause chatter and chipping (see **Figure 4**).

If a tool isn't working as effortlessly as it should, the blade is the obvious place to start looking for problems. A sharp blade will easily slice through paper (see **Figure 5**). This is an almost failsafe, very simple test. A less sensible, yet more traditional, test is to shave hair from the back of one's hand.

In some cases, a cutter may not be addressing the wood at the optimum angle. If a blade cuts deeply on one side of its path and less (or not at all) on the other, the edge may not have been ground square to the sides, or it may be installed in the tool at an angle (see **Figure 6**). Even though it is sharp all the way across, perhaps only a section of it is actually meeting the work.

Figure 1. A sharp plane peels smooth, continuous shavings from the wood.

Figure 2. A sharp chisel slices cleanly across end grain.

Figure 3. Some tools, like this spokeshave, work better pulled instead of pushed.

Figure 4. A plane iron set too deep will chatter and clog.

Figure 5. A sharp blade slides easily through paper.

Figure 6. A cutting edge that is not square to the tool body may interfere with the cut.

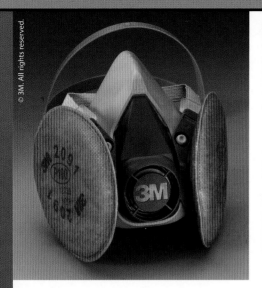

Figure 1-3. The 6291 dust mask from 3M is NIOSH approved, and the company recommends it for occasional metalworking.

Figure 1-4. This dust mask, 3M's 6800, has a plastic face shield for eye protection, which is ideal for turners as well as sharpeners.

Figure 1-5. A powered version of the 3M 6800 mask, the 6800PF, has a battery-operated module that forces air through the filter.

Dust protection

To protect the lungs, nose, trachea (windpipe), and vocal cords from damage when sharpening woodworking tools, there are some precautions to take. The work area should be well ventilated, hands should be washed thoroughly after a sharpening session, and above all, an appropriate dust mask should be worn.

There are a couple of types of dust mask that are appropriate for occasional sharpening. Among the less expensive models is a half-mask from the 3M Company, the model 6291 shown in **Figure 1-3**. According to 3M, this mask is NIOSH (The National Institute for Occupational Safety and Health) approved for environments containing certain oil- and non-oil-based particles. The company recommends it for welding, brazing, torch cutting, metal pouring, soldering, and exposure to lead, asbestos, cadmium, and arsenic. A full-face version of this mask, the 6800 shown in **Figure 1-4**, has a plastic face shield for eye protection. A powered filter version of this mask, the 6800PF shown in **Figure 1-5**, is also available. This is a battery-operated module that forces air through the filter. A further upgrade is the powered ventilator (not just the filter), such as the model shown in **Figure 1-6** from Triton Manufacturing. This adds a hood to fully enclose one's head. A battery powers a pump that provides a continuous stream of fresh, filtered air. Such a system is highly recommended for woodworkers with allergies or previous pulmonary problems or those engaged in more than occasional sharpening, and also for men with abundant facial hair.

Figure 1-6. Systems such as Triton's powered ventilator are highly recommended for woodworkers who suffer from allergies.

Eye protection

In addition to protecting your lungs, it's essential to wear some kind of eye defense, especially when operating bench grinders, power sanders, and automated water stones. Woodworkers who normally wear corrective eyewear can order inexpensive prescription glasses designed for this very purpose. They come with plastic impact-resistant lenses and side protectors that help deflect minute projectiles in the peripheral zone. Nonprescription versions are widely available and inexpensive.

A wonderful supplement to safety glasses is a magnifying headband visor. One version of this device, the OptiVISOR made by Donegan Optical Company Inc. and shown in **Figure 1-7**, comes with an optional light that, in conjunction with the magnification feature, reveals an edge being sharpened in great detail. The visor must be worn over prescription or safety eyeglasses because it has a 2" gap at the bottom, and it does not offer any protection from particles flying upward.

The reason for eye protection is speed. For example, bench grinders operate at either 1725 or more commonly 3450 rpm. On the rim of an 8"-diameter stone, that amounts to a velocity of about 82 mph. Your task is to touch a piece of metal against a stone that is traveling faster than the legal speed limit on an interstate highway.

Wear the safety glasses.

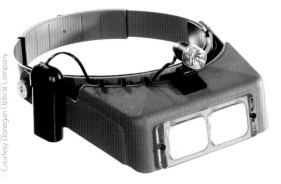

Figure 1-7. Worn with safety eyeglasses, the OptiVISOR and similar magnifiers add a layer of eye protection and also give you a revealing look at the edge being sharpened. This model has an optional headlamp.

A few safety rules

All safety precautions recommended by the manufacturers of grinders and other machines should be understood and followed. While they often look like little more than lawyer's boilerplate, such precautions are often the result of actual experiences and accidents, so due diligence is appropriate.

Common sense also dictates a few basic rules:

- Never thrust a chisel into the path of a revolving stone. Move it toward the stone slowly and carefully.
- Always use the powered grinder's tool rest (sometimes called a toolbar, or a universal support), and any time a jig is available to hold the part being sharpened, use it too. Jigs produce better, more predictable and repeatable results than freehand sharpening, and they're usually safer. Heat travels through conductive metals—if the bit or blade gets too hot, it can burn you, but a good jig usually will protect you.
- Don't touch any power sharpening wheel with your fingers, not even a soft polishing mop or a slow-moving water-cooled wheel. The coolness of the water might feel good, but you'll quickly abrade your skin clean off.
- Don't wear loose sleeves or cuffs while using power grinding equipment, and if you have long hair, put it up so it can't possibly get tangled in the rotating wheel. Wear work boots—you would not want to drop a newly sharpened chisel onto your sandaled foot.
- Be very careful with wire wheels, especially as they age, because individual wires can become airborne at high velocity. And that's just one more reason to wear those safety glasses.

Photo by Author at A & J Supply, Whitewood SD

CHAPTER 2

Introduction to Steel

Sharpening is metalworking. Every cutter, blade, and knife in a woodshop is related in some way to iron, so the logical place to begin learning about sharpening is to have a quick look at the nature, sources, and varieties of iron and its derivatives—steel, carbide, and cermet (ceramics bonded to metal).

The smelting of iron and the processes involved in making it into useful steel combine fire, large machines, and the tough, smart men of the Rust Belt. For all of today's achievements in metallurgy, the iron and steel of the Industrial Revolution are still the most widely used of all metals. Without them, our civilization would grind to a halt.

From iron to steel

In its natural state, iron looks nothing like the shiny steel of a new blade. Because of its molecular makeup, iron can only exist as a compound, mixed with either sulfur or oxygen. In nature, iron oxide looks like caked sand, almost crumbly, with the texture of soft sedimentary rock. In this natural state, it's called ore.

To be useful, iron must first be separated or "extracted" from its bond with sulfur or oxygen. Extraction involves introducing carbon to the ore during a process called *smelting*. There's nothing mysterious here—it is the same carbon found in diamonds, graphite, charcoal, and even the ubiquitous carbon paper. Webster's dictionary defines smelting as "to melt or fuse, often with an accompanying chemical change." The process has been with us since the Bronze Age, when men first learned to combine copper and tin by heating them.

Once iron ore is heated to the point where it becomes a liquid, as shown in **Figure 2-1**, it will dissolve carbon. Therefore, the smelting process is highly dependent on minute changes in temperature. At different levels of heat, carbon and iron combine to create different compounds, which have very different characteristics. Steel usually contains more than 0.05 percent carbon, and yet less than 2 percent. The initial smelting alone doesn't reduce the carbon to these levels—the mill usually follows up with repeated heating and cooling cycles. The usual treatment involves getting the mixture very hot, then cooling it rapidly with either water or oil. It's all about timing—a mill can manage the process to create hard and brittle steel,

Figure 2-1. A huge ladle pours liquid iron ore, hot enough to melt carbon, at the BOP Shop in the Edgar Thomson Works in Braddock, Pennsylvania.

Photo courtesy of United States Steel Corporation

spring steel, or soft, malleable steel, depending on its customers' needs. If nickel and manganese are added, the steel's tensile strength increases. When nickel and chromium are added, the result is stainless steel, and when tungsten is added, the product becomes the familiar high-speed steel of router bits and drills.

Some other definitions might be useful here:

■ *Annealing* means to heat and then cool a piece of tool steel so it becomes soft enough (that is, less brittle) to work. The cooling is usually slowed as much as possible. The annealing process can be adapted to meet several other needs (removing stresses, gases, etc.), but in general it refers to reducing brittleness.

■ *Hardening* is essentially the same process as annealing, except that the steel is quenched (cooled rapidly).

■ *Tempering* or *drawing* refers to reheating the quenched steel and then cooling it at a rate that decreases its brittleness. An inexperienced sharpener often does this accidentally. He or she grinds a chisel or blade to the point that it heats up and becomes blue. Actually, the steel quickly goes through several color changes that are less noticeable than the blue before the change becomes visible—and by the time you see the colors change, the damage has already been done.

One of the largest deposits of iron in the world is located in northeastern Minnesota. After more than a century of mining, the easiest pickings are long gone and the vast Iron Range now harvests taconite, a low-grade ore, in pellet form. Huge hills of small, dark, round, and rusty pellets, each between the size of a pea and a grape, are piled up along the western shore of Lake Superior (see **Figure 2-2**), and especially in the vicinity of the port city of Duluth, awaiting shipment to the blast furnaces (see **Figure 2-3**) of Ohio, Indiana, and Pennsylvania. The region has been supplying

American iron since the late 1880s, and thanks to the Great Lakes, it has always been less expensive to ship the ore to the coal of the furnaces rather than shipping the coal to the range and then transporting the steel back to Detroit and the industrialized East. Today, the range still supplies about three-fourths of America's domestic ore. Although new ore makes up only 40 percent of total steel production, most tool steel comes from that source rather than from the other 60 percent, recycled iron and steel, which (due to impurities) is usually used for car bodies and appliances.

Figure 2-2. Taconite pellets piled high near Iron Mountain, Minnesota, will cross Lake Superior to the steel mills of Indiana and Pennsylvania.

Figure 2-3. Just east of Chicago in Gary, Indiana, U.S. Steel's Number 14 Blast Furnace smelts iron and trace elements into various grades of steel.

Tool steel

While carbide and ceramic are essentially reserved for motorized cutters, most hand tools still use steel knives and blades. This is the material most often sharpened by woodworkers. Called tool steel (see **Figure 2-4**), the metal is extremely tough and resists abrasion, which means it can hold an edge. With low levels of manganese, the carbon content of tool steel is at the middle to higher end of the range for steel, usually around 1 percent or more. Tool steels are a balance between sharpness and impact resistance, and are designed accordingly. Some are destined for use in mattocks (pickaxes and adzes), while others become fine chisels for carving and joinery.

Figure 2-4. Tool steel is widely distributed and is available in sheets, squares, rounds (shown), and other custom profiles.

Common Grades of Tool Steel

Tool steels are uniformly identified by a letter followed by a number. Tool steel usually comes to market as flat bars, round rods, square rods, plates, and sheets. The most common grades of tool steel include the following:

Grade	Characteristics
D-2	Air hardened, high carbon, high chromium, high wear resistance.
A-2	Air hardened, very stable in large diameters or sections.
S-7	Air hardened, high impact and shock resistance.
O-1	Oil hardened, high tungsten and chromium, nondeforming.
O-6	Oil hardened, cold-work steel with graphite carbon throughout.
A-6	Air hardened, nondeforming.
H-13	High in chromium, high impact resistance.

Rockwell hardness test

The hardness of steel is a measure of its resistance to deforming under impact and is measured on the Rockwell scale. The Rockwell method uses either a hardened steel ball (Rockwell B test) or a 120-degree diamond cone (Rockwell C test, more common with woodshop tools). The test takes place in a special small machine which measures how deep the steel is penetrated under pressure, as shown in **Figure 2-5**. The steel is compressed under two different loads, and the difference in penetration between the two tests measures the actual hardness. Essentially, a weight is dropped on the steel and the depths of the resulting dents are measured. The ball is 1/16" in diameter and is used in softer steels. The cone, usually reserved for hardened steel, is a small commercial diamond cut at a 120-degree angle.

The results of the test are given as a number on a scale, which usually runs from 20 to 100. The higher the value is, the harder (and thus more brittle) the steel. Very hard steels, such as knife blades, are in the range of 50 to 60 on the C scale (which is usually written as HRC 50 or HRC 60). Japanese laminated steel blades and chisels are harder than European or American versions, and they usually come in around HRC 65. Softer steel used in tools subject to high impact (for example, those mattocks mentioned earlier) scores lower on the scale. The range is from about HRC 40 to HRC 45.

Figure 2-5. A Rockwell tester measures the hardness of steel by evaluating the depression left by impacting the surface with a small ball or a diamond.

Courtesy Instron/Wilson Instruments

Tungsten carbide

Those expensive carbide tips on table saw blades, router bits, and shaper cutters (see **Figure 2-6**) are simply compounds of carbon and metal. Their cost has steadily been declining since the 1980s, when carbide began to show up in home workshops. The most common compound found in today's woodshop is tungsten carbide. Tungsten (its atomic number is 74) is an extremely hard metal that looks like white steel. It has some amazing properties, including the fact that, of all of the metals available, its melting point is the highest (more than 6,000°F), and it has the highest tensile strength, too. When combined with steel in an alloy, it makes the steel a great deal harder, although also more brittle. Most of the world's tungsten comes from China, but there are important sources in Portugal, the United States, Canada, Australia, Russia, and South Korea, too.

The main reason carbide tips are used in the woodshop is endurance. They hold an edge several times longer than standard high-speed steel (HSS) cutters. In a commercial woodshop, the endurance delivers savings on sharpening costs and also on downtime, while dull bits and blades are being changed out for sharpened ones.

Tungsten carbide blades can be used to cut soft metals such as aluminum and brass, which is useful at times in a woodshop where metal inlays, accents, or hardware need to be fabricated or trimmed to fit a project.

The major downside to tungsten carbide cutters is their brittle nature, and a secondary disadvantage is their cost. Drop a blade on a concrete or steel surface, or run it through old nails, hard knots, or other surprises, and you may see deterioration in the form of minute (or sometimes even quite large) pieces of the cutter edge falling away, as shown in **Figure 2-7**. When it happens, the sharpening shop removes the tip (or insert) and brazes a new tip onto the tool. That brings up the second concern, cost. Tungsten carbide is so hard sharpening it

Figure 2-6. A staple in woodshops, carbide tips are a very hard, fairly brittle compound of carbide and metal, usually tungsten.

Figure 2-7. It may be hard, but carbide doesn't do well when it impacts a buried nail, or is dropped on concrete or cast iron.

requires special equipment—usually diamond-impregnated steel cones, wheels, and hones. While it's possible to sharpen several different kinds of carbide tips in the workshop, most professional shops leave the task to experts.

There are two things to keep in mind about tungsten carbide tips:

First, tungsten carbide tips are so hard they tend to accumulate a buildup of resins over time. Your blade may not be cutting well because it has run so long and become so hot at times that it has collected melted resin from sap, glue, and man-made materials, especially on its sides.

Remove the accumulation and you may find the cutter underneath still has a great deal of life left in it before it requires sharpening. To remove the resin (pitch), soak the tips in citrus oil or lacquer thinner for half an hour, and scrub with a soft brass brush. For circular saw blades, a pizza pan makes a good soaking basin.

Second, tungsten carbide is brittle. That means the cutter must enter the wood at a very large angle, almost a vertical 90 degrees at times. This dissipates the impact across the face of the tip rather than concentrating it along the bevel. The entire tip removes stock rather than just the leading edge. That is important because an inexperienced sharpener may inadvertently change the angle and reduce the efficiency of the tool.

Cermet

What carbide did for woodworkers over the past two decades, ceramics promise to augment over the next few years. Carbide Processors Inc. of Tacoma, Washington, is leading a minor revolution in cutter technology. The company is home to the Northwest Research Institute Inc., where technicians have combined ceramics with metal to produce a new material called cermet, which to the unaided eye looks exactly the same as carbide. In tests, tips made from cermet hold their edge several times longer than carbide tips, which radically extends the interval between sharpening. The other advantage to cermet is that it can accept work at a much higher feed rate than carbide blades, which is of immense interest to industrial wood manufacturers, and also important to small shops producing products like custom hardwood flooring or moldings. Each cermet-tipped blade is custom built at the factory and costs about twice what a tungsten carbide blade costs (which, considering the fact it lasts up to five times as long, may not be such a bad thing). Cermet-tipped blades must be returned to the factory for sharpening.

CHAPTER 3

Introduction to Bench Stones

Most sharpening stones take the form of rectangular blocks that sit on a bench, hence their name—bench stones. The primary options are water stones, oilstones, diamond sharpeners, and, to a lesser extent, ceramics. Some can be purchased in specialized shapes for carving tools and other shaped edges, and some also can be purchased as wheels mounted on a slow motorized machine.

Bench stones primarily are used for honing, that is, creating and refining the small, highly polished bevel that forms one side of the cutting edge. The other side of the cutting edge, also maintained on bench stones, is the flat back of the chisel or plane iron. The infinitely sharp intersection of these two highly refined surfaces is what actually does the cutting.

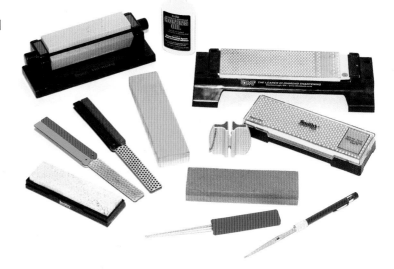

Two bevels

Chisels (and plane irons) have two bevels. In **Figure 3-1**, there's a large, very visible bevel achieved by grinding and a small secondary bevel (often called a micro-bevel) at the tip created by honing. Both grinding and honing involve introducing the blade to a stone. The difference is mainly a matter of degree. Grinding is done with coarse grits, usually at speed, and often on a mechanized wheel. Honing is done with fine stones, more often by hand on a rectangular bench stone, or else on a slow-turning wet wheel. The lines fudge a little between grinding and honing, but many cutting tools have their main bevel ground at the factory and their secondary bevel honed in the shop. While they have a factory edge, it sometimes isn't a very good one. So, the first sharpening step that most woodworkers perform is actually the last one required, honing. That secondary bevel is usually only one to three degrees higher than the primary bevel, so it doesn't take long to hone.

Figure 3-1. Chisels and plane irons have two bevels: a large one formed by grinding and a small one at the very tip formed by honing.

Figure 3-2. Water and oil are cleaners (not lubricants) that float sharpening debris away, preventing the stone from glazing with fine metal residue.

Beyond grinding and honing, sharpeners make another distinction between honing and polishing, the latter being performed on extremely fine stones. There is also an ultimate step, which is stropping on leather or buffing on a soft wheel charged with ultra-fine abrasive. Polishing the flat side of a blade will generally remove the burr created when honing the bevel, which is part of the job of a leather strop.

Choosing a stone

All four types of bench stones—water stones, oilstones, diamond stones, and ceramics—do essentially the same job, and which one you choose is a matter of personal preference. Although there are motorized versions, it's a good idea to begin with the manual versions and learn the dynamics of honing before investing in a machine. As their names indicate, water stones and oilstones use water and light oil as cleaners to float debris away. Diamond stones can be used with either water or oil, though most sharpeners prefer water. Ceramics are often grouped with water stones because they use water as a cleaner,

Sharpening Grits

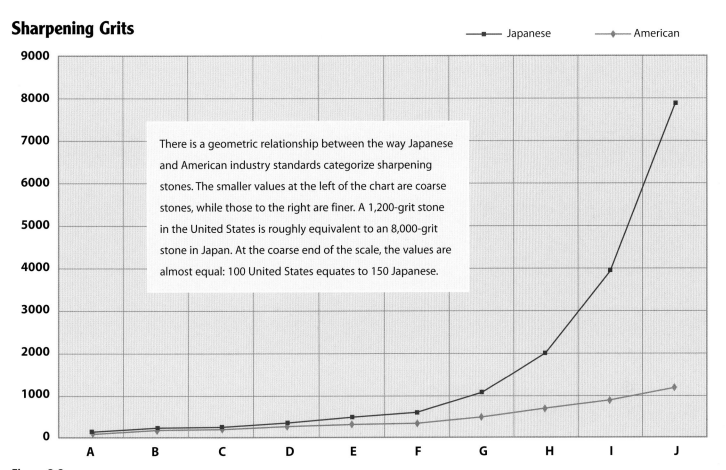

Figure 3-3.

but this isn't strictly accurate. The difference is a water stone typically consists of abrasive particles suspended in a ceramic binder while a ceramic stone typically consists of a powdered ceramic abrasive suspended in a resin binder.

It's tempting to think of oil and water as lubricants, but their main function in sharpening is to float debris out of the way. Both the stone and the blade create debris, and the liquid combines with small particles as they break away from the stone to create a slurry (called swarf), which in turn helps polish the bevel, as shown in **Figure 3-2**.

To look at stones in a simplistic, anecdotal manner, most woodworkers would say diamond sharpeners are the fastest but have some limits at the polishing (very finest) level; oilstones are the slowest but produce the finest edge; water stones lie in between, in both speed and sharpness; and shaped ceramic stones are most suitable for

knives and carving tools, though flat ceramic is now available as well. Any one choice, or a mix, will be quite satisfactory for the vast majority of woodworkers. Those in the know often use a diamond or water stone to hone and an oilstone to polish. This is a very subjective area where being "wrong" probably won't noticeably hurt the quality of an edge. Factors such as cost, ease of use, cleanup, storage, tradition, and brand names, all play a role in your choice.

The stones

Water stones are the traditional honing and grinding tools of the Orient, while oilstones historically are pretty much a European product. Of the two, water stones are more aggressive, but they also wear down more rapidly. Woodworkers have been known to smoke at the ears defending their own personal favorite, but most of us can manage very well on any one of the four primary kinds of stone. Each has its own special qualities. Some cut more quickly but not as finely as others. With modern manufacturing practices, cost differences are no longer as important as they once were. Most professional woodworkers will own some of each type of stone, and almost all will agree choosing the type of stone isn't as important as choosing the right grit.

The Sharpening Grits Graph (see **Figure 3-3**) shows the two grit scales that one is most likely to encounter in oilstones and water stones. The red line describes Japanese stones, while the blue line applies to American grades. To illustrate the difference, the finest Japanese stone that's commonly available is an 8,000-grit abrasive, and its equivalent on the American scale is a 1,200-grit stone. Both are used to gain a highly polished finish. Stones do run all the way up to 15,000-grit on the Japanese scale, but time is money and few woodworkers can afford to spend the extra time required to gain such an exquisite finish because it won't last long if the cutter is used in hardwoods.

Technically, diamond and ceramic stones are sharpeners and not actually stones, but woodworkers, preferring the familiar, have declined to make the jump in terminology. Diamond sharpeners have their own grading system based on microns, and the numbers run in the opposite direction—large numbers are coarse. For example, DMT's 60-micron diamond sharpener is extra coarse, while their 9-micron version is extra fine. (DMT is the brand name of Diamond Machining Technology, Inc., based in Marlborough, Massachusetts.) A micron measures one millionth of a meter, which is $\frac{1}{25,400}$". So, the diamond grit particles on an extra coarse sharpener are actually smaller than $\frac{1}{400}$" in diameter, while those on a 9-micron sharpener are an infinitesimal $\frac{1}{2822}$" wide.

A variety of stones exists within the major categories of oil, water, diamond, and ceramic. The menu can be quite intimidating for anybody new to sharpening, but the following list (see **Figure 3-4**) should help clarify things. It's keyed to the letters along the bottom of the Sharpening Grits Graph in Figure 3-3, and each type of stone is discussed in detail over the next few chapters. The keys (that is, letters) indicate where the stone sits along the line from coarse to fine. Note the names given in the list are generally the manufacturers' designations (which is why some of the "coarse" sharpeners, for example, are listed below some "medium" ones). The list is organized by actual grit, so the coarsest stones are at the top and the finest are at the bottom.

Ref.	Type	Name	Abrasive	Grade	Grit
A.	Ceramic whetstone	Shapton	Ceramic	Extra coarse	120 Japan
A.	Man-made oilstone	Crystolon	Silicon carbide	Coarse	100 U.S.
A.	Man-made oilstone	India	Aluminum oxide	Coarse	100 U.S.
B.	Man-made oilstone	Crystolon	Silicon carbide	Medium	180 U.S.
C.	Man-made oilstone	India	Aluminum oxide	Medium	240 U.S.
C.	Diamond	Monocrystalline	Man-made diamonds	Extra coarse	60 micron/220 U.S.
D.	Man-made oilstone	Crystolon	Silicon carbide	Fine	270 U.S.
D.	Man-made oilstone	India	Aluminum oxide	Fine	300 U.S.
E.	Diamond	Monocrystalline	Man-made diamonds	Coarse	45 micron/325 U.S.
E.	Japanese water stone	Natural stone bonded in ceramic or resin	Coarse		600 Japan
F.	Oilstone	Washita	Natural	Coarse	350 U.S.
G.	Oilstone	Soft Arkansas	Natural	Medium	450 U.S.
G.	Ceramic whetstone	Shapton	Ceramic	Coarse	1000 Japan
H.	Oilstone	Hard Arkansas	Natural	Fine	600 U.S.
H.	Japanese water stone	Natural stone bonded in ceramic or resin		Medium	1200 Japan
H.	Diamond	Monocrystalline	Man-made diamonds	Fine	25 micron/600 U.S.
I.	Japanese water stone	Natural stone bonded in ceramic or resin		Fine	4000 Japan
I.	Ceramic whetstone	Shapton (chisels)	Ceramic	Fine	5000 Japan
I.	Oilstone	Black Hard Arkansas	Natural	Very fine	900 U.S.
J.	Diamond	Monocrystalline	Man-made diamonds	Extra fine	9 micron/1200 U.S.
J.	Japanese water stone	Natural stone bonded in ceramic or resin	Extra fine	6000 Japan	
J.	Ceramic whetstone	Shapton (planes)	Ceramic	Polishing	8000 Japan
J.	Japanese water stone	King stone	Natural	Polishing	8000 Japan
J.	Ceramic	CeraFuse	Ultra White Ceramic	Polishing	7 micron/1500 U.S.

Note: Nagura stone becomes fine slurry when mixed with water and is used on water stones to create a polishing paste.

Figure 3-4. The chart above keys various kinds of sharpener to what type of stone it is, what it's called, what it's made of, where it fits on the spectrum of coarse to fine, and what grit it typically is. The letters in the first column refer to the horizontal axis of Figure 3-3.

The Sharpening Sequence

The complete sharpening sequence proceeds through a logical sequence of steps. However, every cutting edge does not necessarily need to go through the complete sequence every time it is sharpened. It all depends on the condition of the tool and the goals of the sharpener. The complete sequence includes these steps:

- grinding to create the primary bevel,
- honing to flatten the back of the blade,
- honing to create the secondary bevel,
- polishing, or stropping, the secondary bevel and the flat back of the blade.

When to grind

If a tool is damaged along its cutting edge, it's a candidate for grinding (see **Figure 1**). Also, if a tool has been honed several times, it may need a little grinding. Sometimes a new tool has a factory edge that needs work (see **Figure 2**). Other times, a chisel that will be used to chop deep mortises (see **Figure 3**) may need a larger angle than a bench chisel's, achieved by regrinding its primary bevel.

Figure 3. This mortising chisel is being reground to a larger bevel angle.

When to hone

Almost every tool that has been ground needs to be honed. The major exemptions are turning gouges, which are usually ground and then polished, and axes, which usually are left rough. On other tools, begin honing by flattening the back of the cutter (see **Figure 4**) while working through coarse, medium, fine, and extra-fine grits.

Figure 1. The damaged edge of this chisel needs to be ground.

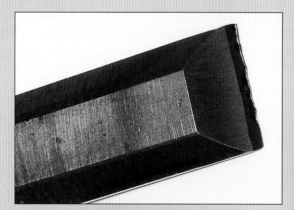

Figure 2. This new tool has a correctly shaped edge, but it is not sharp.

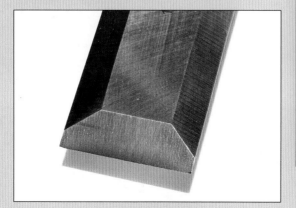

Figure 4. Flatten the back of the chisel on progressively finer bench stones.

To create a secondary bevel on the front of a chisel, set a jig two or three degrees higher than the grind (for example, on a bench chisel go from a 25-degree grind to 28 degrees), and create the thin secondary. The quickest path here is to use diamond sharpeners for coarse, medium, and fine honing and switch to oil or water bench stones (see **Figure 5**) for very fine and extra-fine honing. The job is done when the secondary bevel is uniform and straight all the way across and a slight burr has been raised all the way across the back of the bevel. You can feel it with your fingers. The burr can be removed by honing the flat back of the blade on a very fine stone or by polishing.

When to polish

Polish, or strop, once you have made the secondary bevel straight and uniform, with a slight burr all the way across. Lightly touch the back of a cutter to a charged honing or stropping wheel to remove the burr (see **Figure 6**), and then polish the secondary bevel until there are no scratches. Note that polishing wheels move away from the tool (the tool is below the center of the wheel) while grinding wheels move toward the tool (the tool rest is above the axle). It is very easy to overpolish and make the edge dull, rather than sharp.

Figure 5. Hone the secondary bevel, using a jig to maintain the angle.

Figure 6. Polish the edge by buffing on a charged wheel.

CHAPTER 4

Water Stones

Water stones gained some notoriety in the United States after World War II, when woodworking GIs stationed in Japan began to explore the exquisite traditional joinery of what had been a relatively isolated nation. Opened to the West less than a century before, Japanese architecture had long depended on a woodworking culture that took its sharpening techniques from Samurai swordsmen. During the 1950s, some natural water stones, mined near the ancient capitol of Kyoto, began to find their way to the American market. Since then, they have rapidly gained a following, primarily because they cut faster than oilstones.

Stones from sedimentary deposits in Europe and Japan have been mined for a long time, so the highest-quality, readily accessible material is now essentially exhausted. While a few quality natural stones still are available, they are quite expensive. A less expensive, more viable option is acquiring a man-made water stone. Man-made water stones are fired in a furnace where abrasive material is fused with a bonding agent. They have larger pores between the abrasive particles than oilstones, so they don't clog as easily or become glazed as quickly.

Natural versus man-made

Almost every water stone that one sees in home centers, hardware stores, and woodworking specialty catalogs is man-made. The older repositories of natural stone have been used up, and many of the natural stones coming to the market now are less consistent than one might desire. There are uneven grain sizes and varying degrees of hardness within the same small piece of stone, which makes for some difficult times when honing a wide piece of steel like a hand plane blade. The good news, however, is the man-made versions of the stones are exceptionally uniform, quite inexpensive, and constantly improving. Most are made of aluminum oxide or silicon carbide abrasives, and some are made of ceramic.

Notable exceptions to the declining quality of natural water stones are sedimentary stones from Japan, especially those mined in Narutaki, now a suburb of Kyoto (see **Figure 4-1**). The stones contain fine silica resting in a natural clay host, which produces a relatively soft stone. The surface mines at Narutaki have been serving Japanese woodworkers for about 1,200 years and they, too, have been played out over time. Now stones are brought from beneath the surface via tunnels and are subsequently distributed throughout the woodworking world.

The void in the market left by the shortage of quality natural stones has been more than adequately filled by extremely high-quality man-made water stones, as shown in **Figure 4-2**.

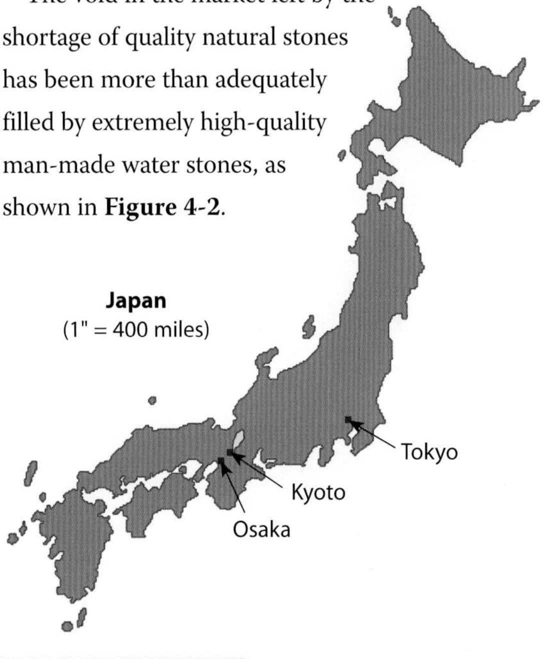

Japan
(1" = 400 miles)

Tokyo

Kyoto

Osaka

Figure 4-1. The finest natural water stones come from the mountains of the Narutaki District, a northern suburb of Kyoto.

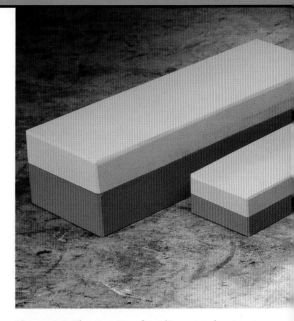

Figure 4-2. The scarcity of quality natural water stones has led to man-made stones, which consist of grit bonded in resin or ceramic. These Japanese-made stones have a different grit on each side.

Figure 4-3. Glaze forming on a bench stone can be caused by insufficient cleaning liquid (water or light oil, depending on the stone).

While they cut faster than oilstones, water stones also wear faster. Some sharpening stones show wear and glaze quickly, as shown in **Figure 4-3**. Natural stones from Japan are generally quite soft and they don't suffer much from glazing, but they do wear. Being soft, they constantly break down and present new facets to the blade. Particles that break off mix with water and steel and become swarf that polishes like a jeweler's rouge. Their softness makes natural Japanese stones easy to restore and flatten, although it also means they wear out quickly.

Natural water stones have traditionally been available in three grit ranges of rough, medium, and finishing. Man-made stones can be more flexible, offering interim grits. For example, Norton water stones are available in four grits—220, 1,000, 4,000, and 8,000. The

Using a water stone

Water stones feel different from oilstones. They resist the movement of the steel, giving the sharpener a clear sense something is happening, a sort of rasping feel and sound. One can sense the resistance, the friction where stone meets steel. The resistance is felt to a lesser degree with diamond sharpeners and hardly at all with oilstones. Perhaps it's due to the different lubricating qualities of oil and water. Whatever the cause, there is satisfaction in it.

Water stones were born in the Orient and have traditionally been used by craftsmen who are sitting or kneeling on the floor, rather than standing over a bench. The advantage of the traditional posture is the craftsman can apply his whole body weight to the action. For a Westerner to use a water stone more easily, the sharpener's body should be at least partially above the stone. This posture can sometimes be achieved more easily if the stone rests on a bench a few inches lower than a standard worktop, which is something to keep in mind when designing your own sharpening station. Something else to keep in mind is the muddy slurry of water stones can make a fair mess, so the sharpening station probably should not be adjacent to your nice, clean workbench. Fortunately, the mud is easy to clean up with water.

Norton Company, a subsidiary of French-owned parent Saint-Gobain Abrasives Inc., has been in the sharpening supplies business for more than a century. Most manufacturers also offer combination water stones, an economical option that combines two grits back-to-back, as shown in **Figure 4-4**.

Just like sandpaper, the salient fact about water stone grits is "more is less." The higher the number, the finer the stone will be. An 8,000-grit water stone is used to polish to a mirror finish, while a 220-grit stone is coarse enough to grind a primary bevel, provided the woodworker has a lot of time and no access to a motorized grinder. A 1,000/4,000 combination stone is a good place to start. It offers a fairly coarse stone for initial honing and a fairly fine stone for finishing.

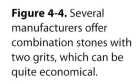

Figure 4-4. Several manufacturers offer combination stones with two grits, which can be quite economical.

Coarse Stones

Water stone sharpening usually begins with the coarser grits (180 to 1,000), but it isn't always true. Quite often an edge just needs a little touchup with a medium stone before the fine work. However, if there are any nicks, chips, gouges, or other damage to the tool, a coarse stone is in order. The most important thing to keep in mind is that a coarse stone can abrade rapidly, which can interfere with, and even reset, the primary bevel. Using a jig to maintain the bevel's angle is essential for beginners. Another advantage to a jig is it avoids making crescents, a rounding of the front edge of a chisel or blade that resembles the arc of a new moon. There are cases where such a result is desirable, but they are the exception— usually you want the sharp edge to be straight across. Begin by adding lots of water to the soaked stone to create a rich slurry. The swarf is essential to the polishing action of the sharpening process. As it thickens, it becomes more abrasive.

Use as much of the surface of the stone as possible while trying to avoid repetitive patterns. Even a figure eight will create grooves, so vary the action with slightly diagonal strokes and straight passes across the stone (see **Figure 4-5**). The key to both a good stone and a great edge is uniform, constant wear.

Before leaving the coarse stone, flatten the back of the blade if this is needed. Avoid overworking the backs of thin blades because their integrity may be compromised over the years. They will become too thin and lose some of their strength.

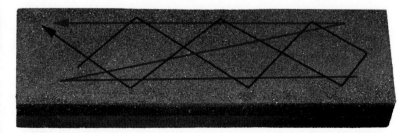

Figure 4-5. To ensure uniform wear on soft water stones, chisels and plane blades should be rubbed against a stone in varying patterns that cover the entire surface.

Figure 4-6. A loupe is a small magnifying glass with a fixed focus (usually 8X), which can be found at office supply houses and photography stores.

Medium-Grit Stones

The function of medium-grit water stones (1,200-grit to 4,000-grit) is to remove any marks left by the coarse stones. A 4,000-grit stone is actually quite fine, but with grits ranging to 8,000 and beyond, it can be classified as a medium abrasive. Begin by checking and flattening the back of the blade if necessary, and then turn your attention to the beveled edge. Maintaining the primary bevel is essential, so using a jig is advisable. When the large bevel reaches a point where you can see no further improvement and the edge is square, reset the jig to address the secondary bevel (see Chapter 9: Angles and Jigs for recommended angles on various tools). A jeweler's loupe, which is a small magnifying glass in a housing that sets the focus automatically, is a wonderful aid at this point. It will reveal a great deal about the quality of the edge. Loupes, like the one in **Figure 4-6**, are widely available from photographic houses and stationers, and they are relatively inexpensive. The OptiVISOR shown in Figure 1-7 on page 5 is also very helpful.

Working the secondary bevel on a medium-grit stone develops a burr along the edge of the tool. When the burr appears along the entire length of the edge, it's time to move up to a fine stone (about 6,000-grit) to remove the burr. People who have been sharpening for a long time have hairless wrists and hands (usually the left ones) because of this step. After they work to remove the burr, they test the blade's edge by shaving the backs of their hands and lower arms. When the edge is fine enough to address hard maple, it's fine enough for barbering, too.

Polishing Stones

At the end of a sharpening session, the polishing stones await. This is a step often skipped by woodworkers. Attaining a dramatically bright mirror finish isn't always necessary, but it can substantially raise the quality of your woodworking and add a great deal of satisfaction to tasks such as paring and fine joinery. Some say the edge on a tool is the measure of a craftsman's skill and dedication, while others appreciate we sometimes have to deliver those shop-built gifts before the holiday is actually over. Somewhere in the middle lies the truth. If one has the time and the inclination, a highly polished edge is most definitely a treasure to enjoy.

Polishing water stones, as shown in **Figure 4-7**, range in grit from 8,000 to 15,000, and most woodworkers are well served at 8,000-grit. These extremely fine stones don't create much swarf on their own because they don't remove much material. To create a polishing slurry, sharpeners use a Nagura stone to make a paste, as shown in **Figure 4-8**. These are small calcium-like stones that are rubbed in circles on the polishing stone and leave a chalky residue which, when mixed with water, somewhat dissolves.

Courtesy Lee Valley & Veritas

Figure 4-7. The very finest water stones (such as the King stone with the chisel on it) can polish a bevel to a mirror finish.

Courtesy Lee Valley & Veritas, and Chris Billman

Figure 4-8. A white Nagura stone (natural or artificial) is used on 4,000- and 8,000-grit water stones to create swarf. Shown is woodworker Chris Billman's sharpening setup, with a Nagura slurry on his water stones.

MIXING OIL AND WATER

A water stone will become clogged and useless if you accidentally use oil on it. The reverse is not true. Some serious woodworkers use water as a cleaner on Arkansas oilstones, although it doesn't work as well as oil.

Care and maintenance

It's essential to secure bench stones. If a stone moves during use, you lose control, and control is critical to a perfect edge. For a method of securing stones, see page 27.

Water stones wear quickly. An oilstone will often last for years without dressing (flattening), but softer water stones wear according to the sharpener's habits and requirements. A woodworker who prefers freehand honing (not using one of the jigs discussed in Chapter 9: Angles and Jigs) will often develop a habit of leaning just a hair to the left or right, wearing the stone faster on that side. And a person who primarily sharpens narrow blades, such as small chisels, is inclined to wear an uneven pattern in the stone more rapidly than one who hones wide hand plane blades.

In addition to bench stones, man-made water stones come in a variety of shapes and sizes to accommodate the profiles of small carving tools and larger turning tools. Specialty catalogs and Websites designed for carvers and turners are good sources for these. If you must use a bench stone to sharpen pointed or narrow tools, try doing it on the edges of the stone. This will avoid wearing grooves in the broad, flat surfaces.

Flattening Stones

A flat water stone is the key to a great edge. Flattening (also called dressing, or lapping) is ideally done at the beginning of every session, but this is hardly practical. Instead, use a steel edge (a try square works well) to check the surface diagonally and also along its length and width, as shown in **Figure 4-9**. If there's daylight below the steel edge, it's time to flatten.

The least expensive way to dress or flatten a coarse- or medium-grit water stone is to attach silicon carbide wet/dry sandpaper (it's usually black) to plate glass using two-sided carpet tape,

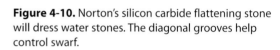

Figure 4-10. Norton's silicon carbide flattening stone will dress water stones. The diagonal grooves help control swarf.

Courtesy Lee Valley & Veritas

creating a lapping plate. (For more on lapping plates, see page 48.) For stones with quite a bit of uneven wear, begin with 100-grit paper and work toward 220-grit. A good sequence here is 100, 120, 150, 180, and 220. Most times, a well-maintained water stone only needs the 180- and 220-grit treatments, and often only the latter. However, having all five grits ready and attached to glass can speed up the process immensely. Complete the final dressing of fine stones with 400-grit paper, using a little water as a cleaner.

After working through the sandpaper grits, rubbing two medium- or fine-grit water stones together can erase any small hollows or bumps that escaped. Stones shouldn't be rubbed together because a coarse stone may abrade and scratch a finer one. Check frequently with your square for flatness. One indication the stone is being flattened evenly is its color will change and brighten as minor scratches and debris in the pores disappear.

An alternative to the relatively inexpensive sandpaper route is to invest in specially manufactured flattening stones, as shown in **Figure 4-10**. The technology has come a long way lately and is very reliable. Dressing stones, also

Figure 4-9. While dressing a stone (that is, lapping, or flattening, it), use a steel straightedge to check for undulation.

Figure 4-11. Water stone edges are brittle, so protect them from crumbling by breaking them gently with a slight chamfer (45-degree bevel).

called flattening stones, are made with a coarse, hard material (Norton's version is silicon carbide). The flattening stone should be secured to a bench before rubbing the water stone across it. Flattening stones are relatively inexpensive and greatly enhance the results of honing with a water stone.

A diamond sharpener can deliver great results as a flattening stone, too. The sharpener should be larger than the stone, and a series of sharpeners running from coarse to fine works best. Use water as a cleaning agent.

The newly flattened stone will have crisp edges, which isn't always a great idea with water stones. They're somewhat brittle, so take some 180-grit sandpaper (or an oscillating machine sander) and gently break the edges just enough to prevent crumbling. Some people round them over, while others create a small chamfer, as shown in **Figure 4-11**.

Water Bath

Beyond flattening, there are several other maintenance issues with water stones. In an environment where the temperature never approaches freezing, coarse- and medium-grit water stones can be stored in a small bath of water, which soaks into their pores and leaves them ready to hone whenever you are. It's best to remove fine- and polishing-grit stones from the water after each sharpening session because otherwise they might clog.

If allowed to freeze, water will crack a stone as it expands while turning into ice.

If a stone is left in a bath of water, a sealed plastic container is a good idea because it prevents, or at least slows, the rate of evaporation, and it also keeps airborne contaminants, such as sawdust, out of the water.

If stones aren't stored in water, they need to be submerged and soaked in water for about half an hour before they are used. Some manufacturers say the stones can be used as soon as bubbles stop rising out of them when immersed, but turning a stone over can often release trapped air, so this may not be the most reliable method. Thirty minutes with a couple of turns is probably the best recipe.

Many professional woodworkers use only distilled or filtered water for their stones, fearing chemicals in tap water. Their worry is probably unfounded, but filtered or spring water is sold in grocery stores. Several manufacturers sell stone baths, which are plastic containers designed to soak and store water stones, as shown in **Figure 4-12**.

Keep in mind that water and fine steel don't work well together, so dry off tools as soon as they're sharpened or rust may become an issue.

MARK THEM
It's a good idea to take a permanent marker and write the grit on every stone as soon as you buy it. It can be hard to tell close grits apart, especially after the factory numbers wear away.

Figure 4-12. The Stone Pond by Veritas comes with a bath, lapping plate, 90-grit silicon carbide for lapping, and clamps on bars to hold the stones for use.

Courtesy Lee Valley & Veritas

CHAPTER 5

Oilstones

Tradition tempers every discussion of oilstones. Until late in the twentieth century, these were the workhorses of American sharpening. Water stones from the Orient were few and far between, and such exotic solutions as diamonds and ceramics were still in their infancy. Oilstones could be quarried in America, and synthetic stones were invented and manufactured here, so they were less expensive, too. The consequence is American woodworking has a great deal of experience with oilstones, and consequently, a high degree of affection for them. One indication of the place they have earned in the common culture is the dictionary lists *oilstone* as a single word, while *water stone* is yet regarded as two separate words.

Hard-wearing, long-lasting, and widely available, many oilstones have been passed down through two or even three generations of woodworkers, and they're still the most common type of bench stone. While sales of other stones are gathering momentum, natural and synthetic oilstones still hold a large share of the market and a special place in many woodworkers' hearts.

Figure 5-1.
Man-made aluminum oxide combination oilstones are quite inexpensive and slower, but harder than, water stones. Use them with sharpening oil, or mineral oil thinned with mineral spirits.

A word about oil

A natural lubricant, oil is used with sharpening stones to clear away debris. It is thicker than water and forms a temporary chemical bond with eroded stone and metal to create swarf. The primary function of oil is cleaning rather than lubrication. It also fills pores in a stone and helps prevent glazing. In a cold environment, oil should be thinned a little to help it perform properly.

There are several oils available commercially, and their weight is designed specifically for sharpening. Motor oil is far too thick. There are various objections to household oil such as WD-40, silicone sprays, vegetable oils, and other common lubricants. Norton, Gatco, Smith, and other suppliers sell well-balanced, high-quality oils for use with natural and man-made oilstones. The oils for oilstones are quite inexpensive and widely available (see **Figure 5-1**). Smith's Advanced Formula Honing Oil is actually a non-petroleum product that can be used on diamond sharpeners, too. It contains a rust inhibitor and cleaning agents.

A less desirable but perfectly adequate substitute is to use mineral oil thinned with about one-third mineral spirits or kerosene.

Natural oilstones

In quarries located primarily in Arkansas, but also in such scattered locations as southern Illinois and Oklahoma, a soft quartz called novaculite is mined to create whetstones for sharpening. In Arkansas, the Ouachita (phonetically, Washita) Mountains are a rich source for several grades of oilstone. Much of the resource is now on federal lands. Novaculite is a sedimentary rock composed primarily of extremely fine-grained crystals of quartz, as shown in **Figure 5-2**. More enduring than water stones, natural Arkansas whetstones are valued more and more as time goes on, even

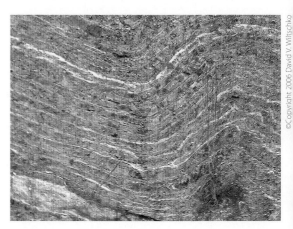

Figure 5-2. The natural oilstone novaculite, a stratified sedimentary rock, can be found in the Ouachita (Washita) Mountains of Arkansas.

as high-quality stone has
become more difficult to
harvest. This very scarcity has,
of course, led to the increasing
use of synthetic oilstones.

Figure 5-3.
Smith Abrasives'
tri-hone system features
six-inch oilstones in fine
Arkansas, medium Arkansas,
and coarse synthetic.

Quarried novaculite quartz
stones are more expensive,
often less uniform, and harder
to find than their man-made
cousins, but a good, quality natural
stone is a true joy to use (see **Figure 5-3**). They
range widely in hardness, and thus in durability.
The hardest are available as either white or black
hard Arkansas stones, with the black varieties
being marginally finer in grit. Color alone is
not a definitive way to determine hardness or
grit—these are natural stones and color varies
tremendously. Softer versions generally inhabit
the middle of the color scale, tending to shades
of gray and green, and while very fine, they
are not quite as fine as the hard stones. At the
coarser end of the scale (about 350-grit), Washita
stones are available in a multitude of colors.
Like ceramics, they are washed with light oil
or an oil/kerosene mix to create swarf, as shown
in **Figure 5-4**. In cold weather, oil works better
if it is cut (thinned) with about 25 percent
kerosene or mineral spirits.

Most suppliers recommend soaking a new
stone in oil for a day or two to charge it. This
fills the pores so that, when used to sharpen,
they don't clog up with steel residue and become
glazed. This works well with coarse stones, but
fine ones won't absorb much oil. They work well
the way they are shipped, as long as they are oiled
frequently during use.

While natural Arkansas stones don't sharpen
steel as quickly as some other options, they
deliver a wonderfully keen edge. They also last a
very long time, so they are an often-overlooked
treasure and a real bargain at estate and garage
sales. Most can be refurbished and saved, as I'll
explain shortly (page 34).

Figure 5-4. While water stones need to be
immersed and soaked, oilstones need only have the
working surface coated with oil.

Man-made oilstones

There are two principal abrasive compounds used to manufacture oilstones: silicon carbide (carborundum) and aluminum oxide (corundum). Both are also used to manufacture grinding wheels, as will be discussed in Chapter 10: Sharpening Machines. In general, silicon carbide stones are coarser than aluminum oxide, and neither material can make a truly fine stone.

Silicon Carbide

Silicon carbide (SiC) stones (see **Figure 5-5**) are classified as oilstones because oil is used to keep them clean. In days past, these were known as carborundum stones, so named by the man who discovered their manufacturing process, Edward Acheson (1856-1931). Founder of the Carborundum Company in the late-1890s (see **Figure 5-6**), Acheson is notable for several major accomplishments in this and related fields.

A native of Pennsylvania's coalfields, Acheson spent his early working years in the employment of Thomas Edison, where he was involved in light bulb technology and the installation of electrical systems in Europe. After leaving Edison, Acheson received numerous patents, many of which were related to his search for a method of manufacturing artificial diamonds. It was during that search that he discovered the hard abrasive he named carborundum.

Silicon carbide oilstones are generally gray in color. Manufacturers often sell them as a block with two or more grits attached to each other. One side of the bench stone will be coarse, while the other will range toward medium, as shown in **Figure 5-7**.

Figure 5-5. Silicon carbide man-made oilstones have become difficult to find in retail outlets, where aluminum oxide reigns.

Figure 5-6. Silicon carbide was discovered by Edward Acheson, founder of the Carborundum Company in the late-1890s.

Figure 5-7. Norton's Crystolon silicon carbide stones are made in an oven at temperatures of up to 2,500°C (about 4,500°F). Silicon carbide is typically gray in color.

The Norton Company sells silicon carbide stones under the trade name Crystolon. Norton's parent company, Saint Gobain of France, also owns the name carborundum.

Commercially, silicon carbide is made in an oven at temperatures of up to 2,500°C (about 4,500°F) by fusing a conglomeration of silica sand with carbon. The resulting crystalline compound can be visually stunning. A multitude of newly created

Figure 5-8. John Rudge's microscopic image of silicon carbide reveals its crystalline structure, myriad facets, and brilliant hues.

facets refract light across the spectrum. John Rudge, a Scottish photographer with a background in biochemistry, has captured this cornucopia of color (see **Figure 5-8**). The hue of the resulting crystals indicates their purity. Yellow and green crystals occur closest to the heat source in the furnace, while blue and black crystals are formed further away. There have been some rare instances of silicon carbide being formed in nature, but all of the bench stones and other sharpening stones of this material are man-made.

Aluminum Oxide

An absorbent white crystalline powder, aluminum oxide is used extensively in industry for such varied purposes as cleaning up liquids and making spark plugs. It's easier to make bench stones with this compound than it is with silicon carbide because its melting point is about 650°C (1,200°F) lower. Aluminum oxide is a chemical bonding of aluminum and oxygen, often referred to as AlOx but chemically Al_2O_3. The stones (which Norton sells under the trade name India stones) are

usually recognizable by their yellow/red/brown color (see **Figure 5-9**). Known as corundum (as opposed to carborundum), the abrasive itself is in the form of hard crystals. Natural forms of corundum include sapphires and rubies. India stones also come in double-sided grits, which

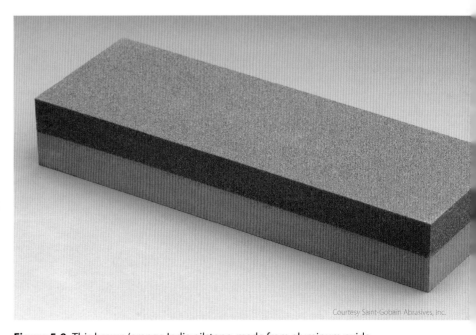

Figure 5-9. This brown/orange India oilstone, made from aluminum oxide, is smoother than quick-cutting silicon carbide.

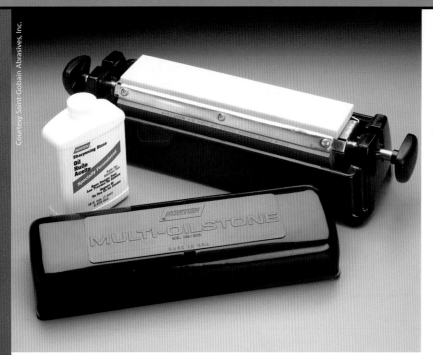

Figure 5-10. Norton's system includes a coarse silicon carbide stone, a medium aluminum oxide stone, and a hard translucent Arkansas stone, all mounted on a triangular bracket.

provide an economical way to purchase them. Norton sells a multi-stone sharpening system called the IM313, which has a coarse silicon carbide stone, a medium aluminum oxide (India) stone, and a fine Arkansas stone attached to a triangular base. The system comes with a plastic oil storage case and reservoir, as shown in **Figure 5-10**.

India stones are lubricated with light oil. They are not available in very fine or polishing grits. For final finishing with oilstones, a natural stone is recommended. Another good choice, discussed in Chapter 6: Diamond Sharpeners, is either a Shapton ceramic whetstone or a CeraFuse ceramic stone.

Reviving old oilstones

There are several cleaners made specifically for removing oils and residue, but I have learned to treat the family to a long movie, wait until the last person leaves the house, and then surreptitiously pop my oilstones and water stones into the dishwasher, as shown in **Figure 5-11**. A standard serving of dishwasher soap works well. After the cycle is completed (and this is why a double feature is a good idea), I open the dishwasher door and let the stones cool for a few hours before moving them (see **Figure 5-12**). You might want to check with your spouse before trying this method.

An older and perhaps more sensible solution is to set an old pan on the stove top (one that will never be used again to prepare food), and heat the stone in water with a dash of dishwashing fluid. To keep the stone from sitting directly on the heat source (the bottom of the pan), pour in a handful of coarse gravel first. Ball bearings are not a good idea because they can cause hot spots. For safety, keep the lid on the pan.

After boiling for 10 to 15 minutes, remove the pan from the stove, rinse the stone well, dump the water, and allow the stone to acclimate and

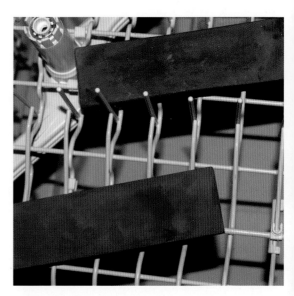

Figure 5-11. Clogged and overloaded oilstones and water stones can be rejuvenated by a trip through the dishwasher prior to dressing.

Figure 5-12. These two stones were garage sale finds, and after a quick restoration, they are now ready for years of service.

Oil or Water? Natural or Man-Made?

The innate strength of natural oilstones is in the finer grits, while synthetics pick up the slack at the other end of the scale. An experienced woodworker who prefers oilstones above other options will probably own a set of five or six. The very coarse stone in this collection will be a synthetic, most probably a ceramic such as silicon carbide or aluminum oxide, which uses oil as a wash. The coarse stone might be either man-made or natural, while the finer stones will all be Arkansas stones: a coarse Washita/soft Arkansas, a medium soft Arkansas, a fine hard black Arkansas, and a polishing stone cut from surgical black Arkansas. Natural stone with very coarse grit is not generally available, and synthetic stones don't compete with the finest natural stones, so a mix of the two creates a better sharpening kit.

There is a general impression among sharpeners, perhaps more anecdotal than empirical, that an oilstone will produce a finer, more polished edge than a water stone. At some point along the road to infinity, that may perhaps be so. However, within the range of reality, both produce an edge that is fine enough for the most demanding woodworker. There is a law of diminishing returns here. One can sharpen an edge too much or at too fine an angle to the point that it becomes brittle and won't last very long. A lot depends on the material being cut, too. Hard, grainy oak resists an edge in a different manner than soft basswood for carving.

cool for a couple of days before working it. If you need to handle the stone, use a kitchen potholder. That will allow moisture to evaporate. Once the stone is completely dry, it can be flattened.

Flattening can be done with a perfectly flat, hard abrasive material. Most commercially available flattening stones are designed for softer water stones, but a diamond sharpener will flatten an oilstone. Begin with the coarsest grit and work down to the finest, using water as a cleaner (see **Figure 5-13**). Let the stone dry thoroughly (several days) before applying new oil.

Some veteran woodworkers use the unglazed (underside) face of a 12" square granite floor tile, while others use dressed concrete. Neither seems like it would be flat or smooth enough, but it's difficult to argue with experience. A lapping plate can do the job, too. Hard oilstones don't respond well, but soft ones will.

It takes time, though. And elbow grease.

Once the stone is clean, dry, and flat, it's a good idea to let it sit for another few days to let any residual water evaporate. At that time, it can be treated like a new oilstone and soaked in oil for a couple of days to fill the pores.

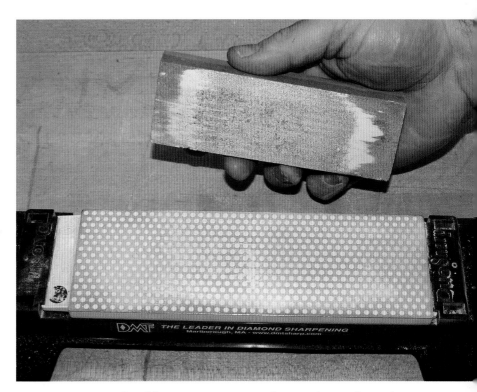

Figure 5-13. Diamonds will flatten water stones or oilstones. They can be used wet or dry.

CHAPTER 6

Diamond Sharpeners

Sharpening systems that employ commercial diamonds are among the newest technologies available to woodworkers. With less effort, less time, and less cleanup than an oil- or a water-based system, a woodworker can remove more metal quicker than with any other non-motorized system.

Diamonds for sharpening are manufactured in two forms: flat plates with a coating of diamond powder embedded in their surface, and diamond paste, a slurry of diamond powder in an oil base that can be spread on a flat plate or a piece of fiberboard of almost any shape. That allows the woodworker to make a diamond hone shaped to suit almost any tool.

Diamond plates

Diamond sharpeners (which, through habit, woodworkers almost universally refer to as "stones") begin with a flat steel plate, which is coated with a softer metal such as nickel. Then, a coating of fine diamond powder is embedded in the nickel. These are essentially the same commercial diamonds used in cubic zirconia jewelry. The abrasive is far harder than even the hardest carbide, so it lasts a very long time. It also is very aggressive, so six strokes can cut as much steel as several times that many strokes on an oilstone or even a water stone.

While they are extremely quick at the coarse end of the scale, some woodworkers observe that diamond sharpeners don't produce as sharp an edge as oilstones in the superfine grits. While this is true when looked at under a microscope, the argument does have a significant hole in it: For most woodworking tasks, a highly polished, superfine edge simply isn't required. For example, many turners use a fine grinder to touch up cutting edges, and they don't even turn off the lathe. When a fine edge is required, the grit size of an extra-fine nine-micron diamond sharpener is pretty much the mathematical equivalent of

Figure 6-2. Being able to sharpen carbide-tipped router bits in the shop is one of the great advantages of diamond sharpeners.

a black hard Arkansas stone (usually the finest stone used in a woodshop). And the industry has developed diamond pastes that take the process all the way down to one micron.

Among the advantages of diamond stones is they require no swarf, as shown in **Figure 6-1**. Neither oil nor water is necessary, although the sharpeners can be cleaned with water and a rag. Many experienced sharpeners do prefer to use a little water because it helps to float away the residue. There is no need to soak diamond stones prior to a sharpening session, which cuts down on prep time. Because of the way they are manufactured, they can literally come in all shapes and sizes. That makes diamonds an ideal choice for sharpening carbide-tipped tools such as profiled router bits and shaper bits, as shown in **Figure 6-2**. In fact, they have essentially replaced traditional files in the world of sharpening because they don't clog or lose an edge. The one disadvantage with earlier versions was they were expensive, but that has improved as the technology has developed, and their exceptional longevity now makes them an excellent investment.

Figure 6-1. Diamond sharpeners can be used dry or with water as a cleaner, and are washed with soap and water after use.

Using diamond sharpeners

Diamond sharpeners are perhaps the easiest stones to use. They are very aggressive, cutting quickly and very evenly, due to their flat metallic base plates. They don't wear quickly, so they don't need to be flattened; in fact, they work well to flatten other stones. Diamond sharpeners don't require wet storage, soaking, applications of oil or water, slurries, or even much cleaning. They seem to be essentially nontoxic, with no apparent health-related issues. For new woodworkers who haven't inherited a set of old oilstones, diamond sharpeners are an exceptional choice for most tasks because of their short learning curve, long life, reliability, and low maintenance. Experienced practitioners will find that the coarser grits save a lot of time, and diamond pastes (see **Figure 6-3**) pick up the slack on the fine and polishing grits.

Diamond Machining Technologies (DMT) is an industry leader in this field, and their plant is located in Marlborough, Massachusetts. DMT has developed the Dia-Sharp Double-X

sharpener, which has a very coarse (120 micron) surface. The aggressive new sharpener is ideal for flattening water stones, ceramics, Arkansas oilstones, and all man-made stones. It is used with flowing water (see **Figure 6-4**), is quite reasonably priced, and offers an alternative to a powered bench grinder without the risk of heat buildup. It can be used to change bevel angles and to remove nicks, chips, rust, and pits.

A rather innovative company named M.POWER has combined DMT diamond sharpeners with a jig that allows woodworkers to quickly sharpen flat blades (planes and chisels). The jig, known as the PSS1 for Precision Sharpening System, holds the blade stationary and its angle constant while

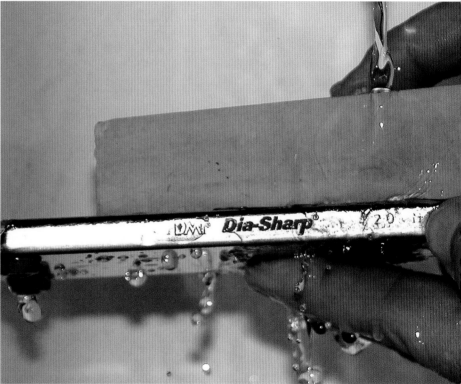

Figure 6-4. DMT's Dia-Sharp Double-X sharpener, with a 120-micron extra-coarse surface, is ideal for lapping water stones. It's meant to be used in flowing water.

Figure 6-3. Diamond paste can be used to lap the back of a plane iron or chisel, using a flat MDF surface and a nonskid mat.

guiding the diamond abrasive across the cutting edge, as shown in **Figure 6-5**. The sharpener travels at a 90-degree angle to the tool's normal cutting direction and holds the cutter at either 25 degrees or 30 degrees, a choice made by the user. The kit includes sharpeners in preparation (grinding) and finishing (honing) grits. When the finish from the finest sharpener looks uniform across the bevel, the back of the tool can be passed across the sharpener once or twice to remove the burr. The jig comes with instructions for use.

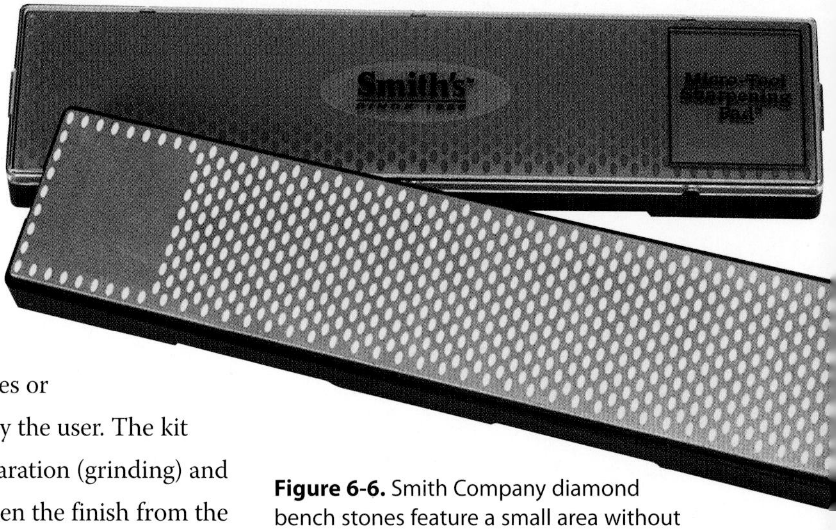

Another innovative leader in the diamond sharpening field, the Smith Company of Hot Springs, Arkansas, offers the standard diamond grid (a series of holes drilled through the base to allow for material movement) with a twist. Several of their sharpeners feature a micro-tool pad, which is a small area on the bench stones that is free of holes. The plate, shown in **Figure 6-6**, can be used for very fine points and blades, which might slip between the grits on a standard sharpener. A similar solution

Figure 6-6. Smith Company diamond bench stones feature a small area without holes, where thin chisels and knives can be sharpened.

is offered by Minnesota-based Rockler Woodworking and Hardware, what sells a set of diamond pocket-sized stones (see **Figure 6-7**) that are ideal for small blades and even carbide router bit touchups. Norton, long a leading manufacturer of sharpening and grinding stones, makes 8 x 3 diamond-coated steel plates that have no perforations, in four different grits ranging up to 1,+200-grit. And Garrett Wade, a leading supplier of woodworking tools, offers an 11"x 4" diamond-coated plate, large enough for the largest of tools.

Figure 6-5. The M.POWER PSS1 uses DMT diamond sharpeners in a clever jig that presets bevel angles at 25 degrees and 30 degrees.

Courtesy Rockler Woodworking & Hardware

Figure 6-7. Replacing traditional files in almost every instance, diamond flats (like this kit from Rockler) are faster, cleaner, and require less maintenance.

Diamond paste

Diamond paste, a very clever innovation, is a sort of slurry wherein minute particles of commercial diamond are suspended in an oil base. It comes in a tube or syringe and easily can be spread on a lapping board, such as ¼"-thick plate glass, and used for final honing. However, the greatest value of diamond paste may be its ability to embed itself in porous surfaces. Spread over the surface of a small piece of MDF (medium density fiberboard), a woodworker can create custom-shaped whetstones in the shop. The fiberboard can be milled and shaped to fit the contour of almost any carving or turning chisel, then soaked in diamond paste. With use, the paste base migrates below the surface, and the diamond particles rest close to the top. Such a stone can be reused, and indeed refreshed, many times over.

Hartville Tools offers a diamond paste honing kit, which they suggest using as the final step after a regular sharpening routine. According to the company, polishing with diamond paste produces a mirror finish on chisels and plane irons that are used to work wild- or difficult-grained woods or to do fine paring. They suggest using a smooth, flat block of a close-grained hardwood such as hard maple as a substrate for the paste. Use one grit per block, and store the blocks separately to prevent cross-contamination of grits. The kit comes with an instruction sheet, which says that diamond paste may be used as a fine hone and polishing grit after water, oil, ceramic, or diamond sharpening.

CHAPTER 7

Ceramic Sharpeners

A ceramic is an inorganic, nonmetallic material created by the introduction of extreme heat. It can be natural or man-made. The most familiar versions have been with us for millennia, taking the form of glazed pottery and jewelry. Over the past fifty years, the technology of ceramics has taken dramatic strides and a whole new industry has developed around their culture and improvement.

So far, two companies have made significant strides in introducing ceramic sharpening to the woodworking world. DMT (Diamond Machining Technologies) has created knife sharpeners that are of interest to carvers and whittlers, while the Shapton Company has elevated sharpening with ceramics to an art form. Many other companies offer products targeted at other markets but may find a home in woodworking. Like diamond sharpeners, ceramic stones will successfully hone carbide-tipped tooling.

Figure 7-1. Various manufacturers supply pairs of ceramic rods, which are an excellent choice for sharpening household knives.

Courtesy A.G. Russell

Composition of ceramics

There are essentially three types of ceramic. Those that bond with oxygen are called oxides and include alumina and zirconia (manufactured diamonds). Nonoxide ceramics include borides, carbides, nitrides, and silicides (silicon-based). Then there are ceramic composites, which combine the two other categories. Some ceramics conduct electricity; they are known as semiconductors, and some are superconductors.

The most interesting aspect of the materials is their heat resistance, which is the key to their use in sharpening. For the woodworker, it's comforting to know ceramic sharpening materials can handle a lot of heat. Excess heat is the number one problem in sharpening.

The stones are created using a hardened ceramic powder, which is suspended in a resin binder. With their crystalline structures, ceramics tend to be brittle, and their reaction to impact is to shatter rather than to crack or crumble. The resin binder, however, adds resilience and allows ceramics to be formed into a wide variety of shapes, as shown in **Figure 7-1**.

While all man-made oilstones are, strictly speaking, ceramic in nature, there is a distinction between them and stones actually marketed as ceramic whetstones. One important difference is the ceramic stones use water, not oil, as a cleaner. They are designed to combine fast-cutting action with low maintenance. They are not designed to require immersion or soaking in water, but rather need just a small spray of water every now and then during use. Oil is most definitely not recommended.

Some Japanese water stones are manufactured with natural stone embedded in a ceramic base. These are referred to as water stones, not ceramic stones, because only the base (not the abrasive) is ceramic.

Ceramic products

Shapton's GlassStone series, with grit sizes from 220 to 30,000, is a combination of ceramic abrasive on tempered glass (see **Figure 7-2**). The stones are incredibly uniform and a joy to use. Shapton also offers the high-quality Professional Series, which is available in grits from Japanese 120 all the way up to 30,000. Most Shapton stones come with a plastic combination base and storage case.

Figure 7-2. The Shapton ceramic sharpening system requires a little practice and patience, but the stones are very uniform and the results are very impressive.

Courtesy Shapton® Stones

Figure 7-3.
Harrelson Stanley's
DVD is a well-scripted,
well-organized guide
to the Shapton ceramic
sharpening system.

Shapton's Harrelson Stanley appears in a DVD released in 2005 (available through the company's Website; see supplier appendix on page 150), which introduces his "side sharpening" technique (see **Figure 7-3**). The one-hour movie explains in detail how to use Shapton ceramic stones and is a valuable guide for anybody interested in using almost any type of bench stone to sharpen woodworking tools and cutters. The results he achieves are very impressive. One salient point he makes is that a lapping stone can be used frequently during sharpening to maintain perfectly flat abrasive stones.

Other manufacturers offer ceramic stones (aluminum oxide abrasives embedded in ceramic) in grits from 600 to 1,200. The stones, fused at extreme temperatures, use neither oil nor water as a cleaner, although a damp cloth can be used to wipe them.

DMT offers a line of ceramic sharpeners using their patented CeraFuse process, which the company says "transforms the surface of aluminum to an extremely hard, dense aluminum oxide that has the same properties as solid ceramic materials (see **Figure 7-4**). With a finer grit than bonded diamond products, they are unbreakable, wear resistant, light, and nonporous." Of particular interest to carvers is DMT's Diafold ceramic serrated knife sharpener (see **Figure 7-5**), which hones small gouges and fixed or folding knives. It is equipped with a 4" ceramic rod, and it measures just 9½" (240 mm) open and 5" (125 mm) closed. The taper runs from ¹⁄₁₆" to ¼" (1.6 mm to 6.4 mm).

Figure 7-4. CeraFuse is a hard, dense aluminum oxide with the properties of ceramic and a finer grit than bonded diamonds.

Figure 7-5. Of particular interest to carvers is the DMT Diafold ceramic knife sharpener, which is ideal for small gouges.

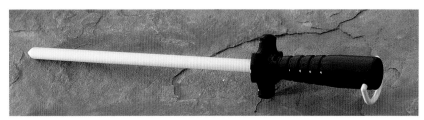

Courtesy DMT®, Diamond Machining Technology

Also available is a traditionally shaped steel (see **Figure 7-6**), which has a ceramic rod that is ideal for sharpening household knives. As the technology continues to accelerate, it shouldn't be too long before a large part of the sharpening market employs ceramics in a myriad of new ways.

Figure 7-6. DMT's unbreakable ceramic steel has a 7-micron grit and is manufactured using the patented CeraFuse process.

CHAPTER 8

Sandpaper and Leather

Surprisingly, sandpaper is an effective and legitimate (although not very economical) sharpening agent. Because it comes in the form of sheets, belts, or disks mounted on various machines, it can be used in a variety of ways to grind and hone. The key, as with all abrasives, is to avoid an excessive buildup of heat. That could suggest that the only sandpaper to use is wet/dry silicon carbide (usually black or gray) paper and to repeatedly douse it with water. But this is not so at all. Almost every type of paper has a use. It just depends on the application.

Leather strops and buffs are used to put the final polish on a sharpened edge. Strops traditionally were flat pieces of leather, but now they come as wheels, too. Buffs are usually cotton and come as stitched wheels where the stitching frequency determines how stiff and hard they are. Both are generally charged with one of several polishing compounds to increase their abrasive abilities.

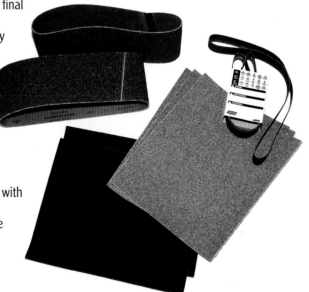

Lapping

Perhaps the best use of sandpaper in sharpening is lapping. Many hand tools require more work than simply sharpening the edge. For example, the bottom (sole) of a hand plane must be completely flat before it will operate efficiently, no matter how finely the blade has been honed. Sandpaper is an excellent way to flatten (lap) the sole.

The first step in lapping is to create lapping plates, which are simply flat surfaces coated with sandpaper, as shown in **Figure 8-1**.

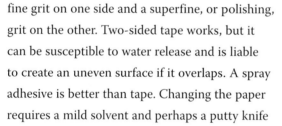

Figure 8-1. Wet/dry sandpaper attached to plate glass creates a flat surface for flattening plane soles and the backs of chisels and plane irons.

They can be made by gluing a few sheets of wet/dry sandpaper onto two pieces of plate glass. One piece of glass will have a coarse grit on one side and a medium grit on the other (see **Figure 8-2**). The second plate will have a fine grit on one side and a superfine, or polishing, grit on the other. Two-sided tape works, but it can be susceptible to water release and is liable to create an uneven surface if it overlaps. A spray adhesive is better than tape. Changing the paper requires a mild solvent and perhaps a putty knife because the adhesive sits on top of the glass rather than penetrating it.

A good series to follow in lapping is 80-, 120-, 220-, and 400-grits, although planes in good condition may prefer 220, 400, and 600. Use a water-resistant felt marker to draw some lines across the sole (see **Figure 8-3**), and then start with the most aggressive paper. Work down to the finest grit, using plenty of water as a cleaner. The marker lines will reveal your progress through the grits. Don't remove the blade. Just retract it so that it doesn't protrude below the sole. Leaving it in place (and under mild pressure) stabilizes the plane body and stops it from warping. If the sole was lapped without a tensioned blade and one is later inserted and tensioned, the body may twist the sole out of flat.

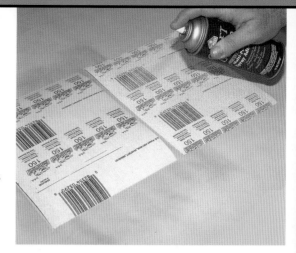

Figure 8-2. A spray adhesive works well to attach sandpaper to glass for a lapping plate, and allows for easy removal, too.

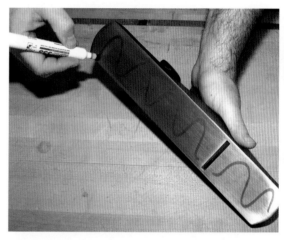

Figure 8-3. Before lapping, draw felt marker lines on the plane's sole. Lapping until they are completely erased indicates flatness.

Figure 8-4. The natural stance when using a plane works well during lapping because it spreads force fairly equally across the sole.

Rub the tool back and forth across the lapping plates, as shown in **Figure 8-4**, until you feel the sole is flat, checking the felt pen marks as you go. Use a steel straightedge to visually check your progress.

Lapping plates are also handy when it comes to the first step in actual sharpening. The back (unbeveled) face of a blade must be as flat as the sole of the plane and as smooth as the micro-bevel itself, at least in the area of the edge. In addition to lapping the soles of hand planes, you would also lap the flat back faces of plane irons and chisels. Beyond lapping, sandpaper lapping plates also can be used to grind and hone, just as if they were bench stones.

The truth about grit

While all woodworkers are familiar with sandpaper, they may not be so familiar with the individual elements that make up the product. The word "grit," when applied to sandpaper, indicates the size and density of abrasive particles. Higher numbers indicate finer grits. Small numbers like 36 and 60 indicate large particles, so less of them will fit in a square inch. These, therefore, are coarse grits. High numbers such as 400, on the other hand, are fine grits. There are very specific guidelines on grit density provided by such bodies as the Unified Abrasives Manufacturers' Association (UAMA) in America and the Federation of European Producers of Abrasives (FEPA) in Europe, which is more international in nature. While the organizations have developed highly technical standards based on measuring the actual size of the particles (in terms of an average or a range, respectively), it's enough for woodworkers to know the grit number simply indicates the density of particles per square inch. It doesn't mean the literal number of particles. In the macro-photograph of garnet paper shown in **Figure 8-5**, for example, the number of particles on 50-grit paper is about 1,500 per square inch.

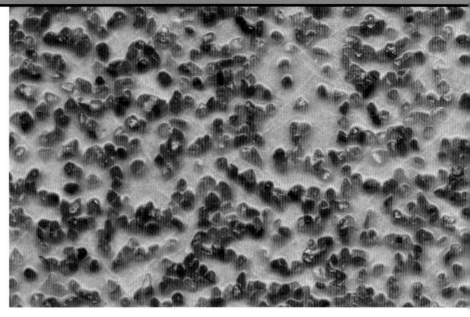

Figure 8-5. With 1,500 particles per square inch, 50-grit natural garnet paper is an open coat sandpaper that won't clog quickly.

Grits range from 12 to 2,500 and beyond, but woodworkers who sharpen with sandpaper tend to use a range of 50 (very coarse) to 400 (very fine). Working through the grits on most woodworking projects, one would use a selection such as 120, 150, 180, and 240, depending on what is available. Sanding sealer is often touched with 320-grit, and 400-grit wet/dry paper is a popular choice between coats of finish. The density (specific gravity/hardness) of the wood species being sanded, the abrasive material being used (aluminum oxide, garnet, emery), and personal preferences all play a role. Over the years, woodworkers become comfortable with their own choices in this area, some of which include other abrasives such as steel wool, pumice, and even culinary pot scrubs. Their experience with abrading wood tends to influence their choices in using sandpaper to abrade steel.

Coarse grits tend to be open coats, where there is some space between the particles (up to half the area in some cases), to help them resist clogging with debris. Fine-grit papers are generally closed coats, with little, if any, space between the particles. Fine papers remove very small pieces of wood (or, in the case of sharpening, steel) and are thus less likely to clog quickly. Wet/dry papers are designed to use water as a cleaner and lubricant.

Paper, or backing

The word "paper" in sandpaper is a loose term, covering various types of backing materials. These include cotton and man-made cloth, as well as Mylar and other fibrous compounds. Mylar, according to the DuPont company, is "an extraordinarily strong polyester film that grew out of the development of Dacron in the early 1950s." Mylar is generally reserved for the finest grits because of its tight structure. Old-fashioned wood-fiber paper is used to back sheets that won't encounter water, and fabric backings (usually polyester or nylon) are more likely to appear in belts and disks, where they are often layered for strength, and in wet/dry papers.

Backings are categorized by weight, and this can be confusing. Both paper and fabric manufacturers use letters to describe the different weights, but in paper the letters are sequential, while in fabric they are not. From light to heavy, the weights in paper are A, B, C, D, E, and F, while in fabric they are M, T, Y, X, and J.

Choosing the right backing is important in sharpening because a woodworker often needs to use water as a coolant, and standard paper doesn't hold up long when wet. The weight of the backing is critical, too. Very fine papers often come on very thin backing, and while this works well for sanding softwoods, it is not ideal when it comes to sanding steel. At the other end of the scale, it's possible to choose a product with a backing so heavy it is inflexible, which restricts its use. For example, a paper with a heavy backing can't be rolled to the shape of a gouge, as shown in **Figure 8-6**.

Figure 8-6. Fine wet/dry sandpaper wrapped around a dowel is a simple way to remove the burr on the inside of a gouge.

Sandpaper sizes

The standard size of a sheet of sandpaper is 9" x 11". Many suppliers also offer one-quarter- and one-third-sized sheets to fit electric sanders. Custom sizes are easy to order from most manufacturers.

Sanding belts come in an array of sizes designed for specific machines. Note: the joint on some belts means they can only run in one direction. If there's an arrow printed on the back (inside) of the belt, it indicates the forward direction and the lapped joint may come apart if the belt is installed the wrong way around.

Disks come in 3", 4", 5", 6", 8", 9", 10", 12", 15", and other diameters. (Despite the industry's widespread use of "disc," the dictionary prefers disc to describe electronic media, and "disk" to describe round, flat objects.) Other sandpaper formats include cords and tapes, which have minimal uses in sharpening.

Abrasives

Perhaps the most familiar (although not the most popular) coated abrasive on sandpaper in the woodworking world is traditional garnet, a natural material that is usually an orange/red/light brown color, as shown in **Figure 8-7**. Natural garnet, which is used as a gemstone, appears in almost every color except blue. Although it is the January birthstone, garnet is quarried far more for industrial abrasives use than as a gem. The advantage of garnet is it breaks down in use, exposing new, sharp edges. This is also its disadvantage—it wears more quickly than some other materials.

Also familiar to most people is emery (the same material used to manicure fingernails), which usually appears as a black paper with a fabric backing and finds more use as a polisher than as a grinder due to its fine particle size. Alumina zirconia and silicon carbide also find their way onto sandpaper, as does crocus, a very fine iron oxide used in the gold industry as a polishing agent. The electronics industry still uses flint in a

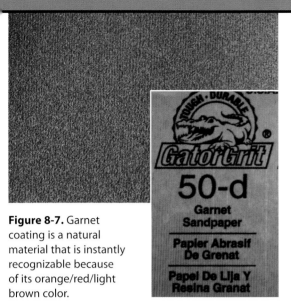

Figure 8-7. Garnet coating is a natural material that is instantly recognizable because of its orange/red/light brown color.

limited fashion for abrasive chores because it doesn't conduct electricity. However, the most common abrasive is the same gray aluminum oxide used to manufacture man-made oilstones, as shown in **Figure 8-8**. Like garnet, aluminum oxide is a friable material, which means it breaks down with heat and pressure, and constantly presents new, sharp, fragmented edges. That makes it consistently sharp, and unlike garnet, it is quite durable.

Gray/black-colored silicon carbide is also used to make sandpaper, primarily of the wet/dry variety; this is. Harder than aluminum oxide, silicon carbide is somewhat better suited to abrading steel during the course of sharpening, and the wet/dry backing is a real boon. Silicon carbide, too, is friable. However, it tends to wear a little more quickly when used on wood and soft metals. Aluminum oxide and silicon carbide are relatively coarse grits in the world of oilstones, but when it comes to sandpaper they can be quite fine.

Ceramic is the hardest commercially viable paper abrasive. It comes in coarse grits and can be quite expensive. It is useful for grinding because it usually comes in belt form and has a high resistance to heat buildup.

Other coating compounds use various elements such as man-made diamonds, chrome (used in extremely fine micron-rated polishing papers and cloths), and various aluminum compounds, all of which are spread or embedded into specialized sandpapers designed for industrial applications.

One other specialty abrasive worth mentioning is stearated paper, which is sandpaper with a built-in lube (actually, a sort of soap) that helps prevent clogging. It is usually reserved for sanding between coats of finish rather than as a sharpening agent, although it does have some specialized uses in the industrial sharpening world.

Bonding

Abrasives must be bonded, or stuck to the backing, to be useful. This is a tricky area because many liquids that attach successfully to both fabric and abrasive will have molecules that are as large as, or even larger than, the fine abrasive particles. They would, in effect, drown the abrasives, and only the bonding agent would come in contact with the steel. Other issues include heat resistance (many adhesives fail when intense heat is generated by abrasion) and water resilience. Urea and phenolic resins have replaced traditional hide glue as the bond on most sandpapers. Resins resist both heat and water better than glue does. That makes modern wet/dry sandpaper much more suitable for sharpening than older, glue-based papers.

Figure 8-8. Most sandpaper products available in a hardware store are coated with aluminum oxide abrasive.

By permission, Ace Hardware, Spearfish SD

Figure 8-9. Leather strops, usually chucked in a drill press, run at low speeds and are charged with very fine abrasives.

Stropping and buffing

Sharpening usually begins with grinding, generally advances to honing, and sometimes requires one more step: polishing. Fine polishing can be done with leather (stropping) or with a fabric or paper wheel (buffing). In both cases, the actual polishing is done by a very fine abrasive that has been applied to the strop or the buff. The leather or the paper wheel becomes the somewhat resilient conveyor of the abrasive material.

A stropped edge usually doesn't last very long because it is essentially the finest edge that normal sharpening procedures will achieve. On the plus side, stropping takes only a few seconds, so it can be done repeatedly. This is a common practice among carvers and turners.

Widely available and quite inexpensive, leather can polish a honed edge to a very fine finish. Leather strops come in numerous forms, from

Figure 8-10. Some slow wet sharpening machines offer shaped leather strops to polish the edge created on their grindstones.

Courtesy Scheppach GmbH

belts and motorized disks (see **Figure 8-9**) to small pieces that are glued to shop-made wooden backers. The most popular method for stropping woodworking tools is to use a leather wheel in a drill press, in a portable drill, or mounted on a designated machine, as shown in **Figure 8-10**.

There are various fabric and paper wheels available for buffing. One of the best suited to buffing woodshop tools is Grizzly's H1393, which is an 8" x ½" x ½" laminated sisal wheel. Rated for 4,000 rpm, it will work on most bench grinders. It is used to buff tool steel, stainless steel, copper, aluminum, and brass. According to the company, the sisal removes small scratches, while the cloth gives a fine finish.

Buffing compounds

Leather alone will quickly strop an edge, and indeed this was the traditional method, but it can heat the edge quickly and requires a fair amount of effort. Applying a buffing compound or a diamond paste accelerates the process, and ultra-fine grits will polish to a razor edge. The compound, rather than the leather, does most of the work, so the blade stays cooler. Unlike leather, cloth buffing wheels will not strop an edge on their own; they must be used with buffing compound.

It is extremely important to designate just one compound for each strop or buffing wheel and to clean tools between grits so as not to contaminate the next strop. The compounds must not be mixed, or they will all become coarse grits. One way to avoid the problem is to settle on a single compound, such as Flexcut Gold (see **Figure 8-11**), which will satisfy the vast majority of a woodworker's needs.

Different manufacturers use different methods to describe the grit level of a buffing compound, but, in general, the most aggressive is black emery, then white or brown (tripoli), followed by yellow (gold), then Zam (or zip), and finally white and red rouge. These are marketed primarily to jewelers and lapidarists for polishing

Figure 8-11. Flexcut Gold is a blend of aluminum and titanium oxide, for a balance between aggression and a high polish.

Figure 8-12. Sets of buffing compound usually include a range of coarse emery, tripoli, white rouge, and fine red rouge.

precious metals and stones. Dremel markets a very nice package called the All-Purpose Buffing Compound Set that includes four five-ounce bars, one each of emery, tripoli, white rouge, and red rouge (see **Figure 8-12**).

Stropping and buffing technique

The problem with stropping, and especially when a machine is involved, is knowing when to stop. The idea is to achieve a bright finish and to stop before reaching a mirror finish. The resilience of the buffing wheel means that too much stropping will actually round over an edge and make it dull.

A tool must be pulled across a strop rather than pushed as on a bench stone. This is true whether the strop is manual or mounted in a machine such as a drill press, as shown in **Figure 8-13**. Strops can be custom-made to conform to the various shapes of carving tools, or they can be purchased already formed (see **Figure 8-14**). Shaped strops are often called "slips," from the older practice of using shaped stones (slip stones) to touch up curved and profiled blades.

The difference between a slip and a strop is the former is often made from medium density fiberboard or a similar wood product, while the latter is almost always leather. Slips can be used first to sand and then to polish. Simply line the slip with the right grit of sandpaper to use it as a shaped sander.

Several companies sell contoured leather wheels for grinders that are factory shaped with concave, convex, straight, and beveled profiles. And some turners like to install a leather strop (wheel) directly on the outboard side of their headstock, if the lathe is so equipped, so they can frequently polish the edges of skews and gouges without shutting down. Others believe that method is unsafe as the work is still rotating and applying pressure can interfere with the rotation, causing run-out, or because stropping at several different speeds is an unsound practice. A wiser solution might be to locate a slow grinder equipped with a leather strop next to the lathe.

Figure 8-13. A tool must be pulled across a strop or a buffing wheel rather than pushed. That is true on both manual and powered strops and buffs.

Figure 8-14. The Flexcut SlipStrop is molded for polishing and deburring V-tools, gouges, and outside edge bevels.

CHAPTER 9

Angles and Jigs

Although there are customary angles for the ground bevels on edge tools, the "correct" angle is subjective, determined by the woodworker's preferences and the task at hand. Jigs offer a good starting place. They generally deliver a bevel that needs little tweaking. Given that, most woodworkers prefer to use a jig when grinding the primary bevel and honing the secondary bevel because the jig reduces guesswork and offers a lot of control.

Some tools, such as Japanese planes and chisels, are not sharpened in the same manner as standard Western tools. And some woodworkers add a back bevel to tools used in highly figured wood. In such cases, jigs may or may not be useful. That discussion, and others related to jigs, usually begins by taking a look at angles.

Sharpening angles

Sharpening angles are subjective. There is no magic number that describes the one angle to which all bevels should be ground. If one were to give identical hand planes to several master craftsmen, no two would grind exactly the same bevel. Issues such as tradition, the specific gravity and grain patterns of the wood species to be worked, and the hardness of the steel all play a role in their decisions.

Other variables abound with other hand tools. For example, one woodworker holds a chisel at a definable angle to pare a sliver, while another is a degree or two different because of his/her stance, hand size, and physical height, the length of the chisel, the height of the workbench, and so on. The best we can do is to determine an average and then suggest some standard deviations to accommodate the vagaries of humanity.

When it comes to machine cutters, things are much more focused. For example, jointer and planer knives have factory-recommended bevel angles. But even here, there is room to maneuver. And some advanced woodworkers add a back bevel on jointer knives and plane irons to work figured grain (more on this on page 62).

One saving grace with hand tools is there is a built-in quotient of error. A degree or two difference in the bevel angle, in either direction, is rarely critical. If a chisel isn't cutting quite the way it should, changing the bevel angle or the blade angle isn't a monumental task. This is not true with most planes, which come with the angle of the blade already set (see **Figure 9**-1). There is only the option of changing the bevel angle, and in the case of bevel-down bench planes, of adding a second bevel on the flat back face of the iron.

Sharpening is akin to cooking. Two chefs given the same ingredients can turn out two very different dishes, both delicious. While we aim for a particular set of angles, sometimes that ideal needs to be adjusted to suit our habits and the environment. So, follow the recipes given below, and be prepared to alter the spices to suit your own taste.

Pitch and bevel

There are two ways in which a cutter can contact the work. In one, the cutter is the tool (gouges, chisels, and knives), and in the other, the cutter is installed in a tool (planes, spokeshaves, and jointers). In both cases, the angle of the bevel is engineered to take into account the angle at which the cutter meets the work. This is variously called the angle of address, the cutting angle, or a lesser-used term such as the prime angle. A chisel may have a bevel ground at 25 degrees, and if a woodworker holds it at another 30 degrees, it actually contacts the work at 55 degrees.

Figure 9-1. A block plane has an acute pitch (in the region of 20 degrees) because the iron is inserted with the bevel up.

20°

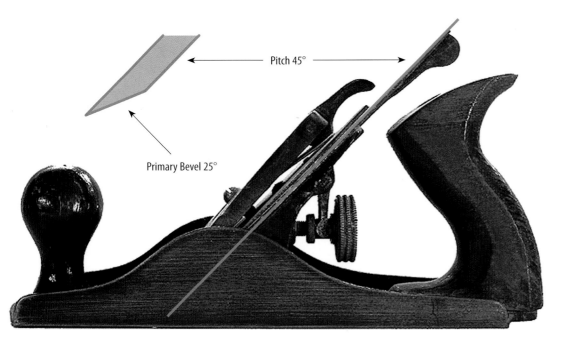

Pitch 45°

Primary Bevel 25°

Figure 9-2.
The pitch on a jack plane is around 45 degrees, and because the bevel faces down, the bevel angle is not as crucial as it is on a block plane, where the bevel faces up.

For simplicity's sake, we shall call 55 degrees the included angle and refer to the 30-degree angle as the pitch.

With direct (hand-held) cutters, the pitch can fluctuate dramatically, depending on the work and the worker. With indirect applications, such as with planes, the pitch is locked (see **Figure 9-2**). That is, the blade usually meets the work at the exact same angle. The blade (iron) can be removed and replaced at precisely the same pitch.

Determining the optimum angle for a bevel begins with the original factory setting. From there, one can experiment by opening or closing the angle a few degrees, by adding a back bevel (see page 62), or even by crowning the front edge of the blade to give it a tiny "smile" so that the corners don't leave lines on the wood of wide boards, as shown in **Figure 9-3**.

Figure 9-3. Planes used to flatten wide boards often have an iron ground with slightly rounded corners, or a gentle arc.

Changing the bevel angle

The main reasons to deviate from the original bevel settings are grain patterns (the amount and directions of figure), mill cuts (plainsawn, riftsawn, or quartersawn stock), the specific gravity of the species being worked (light or dense), and the quality of the cutter's steel. Over a lifetime of woodworking, other reasons will evolve, but a good rule of thumb is to make the angle higher for more difficult work.

Intricate figures can really only be tackled by honing and polishing the blade to an extraordinarily fine edge. Changing the bevel to a higher angle definitely helps, and a back bevel can help, too. But if the leading edge isn't true, flat, and fine, nothing else will work. The blade should be honed to 8,000-grit and then very quickly stropped with an extremely fine compound. The grain should be tackled at an angle, as shown in **Figure 9-4**. The side of the plane doesn't have to be parallel to the edge of the work nor to the tool's direction of travel. Angling it left and right may aid in creating a clean cut. The idea is to slice rather than tear, and approaching at an angle may help.

Figure 9-4. Holding a plane at an angle while moving it along the grain can slice the wood fibers and help tame wild grain.

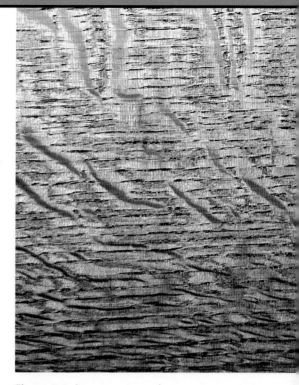

Figure 9-5. Some species and cuts present unique problems for hand planing, where nice, tight grain is mixed with figure.

Cabinet scrapers are a wonderful solution with wild grain, too. They remove the wood fibers by scraping with a sharp burr, rather than by slicing with a sharp blade, and consequently, they are less likely to tear the fibers from the surface.

Mill cuts often call for compromise. Quartersawn and riftsawn stock usually planes and cuts rather well because the tight, linear grain is ideally suited to a straight-on approach with a standard plane. The cutter just needs to follow the grain. Some species with a lot of flake (ray cells) may present difficulties in these cuts, but in general, quartersawn stock (see **Figure 9-5**) planes well. Plainsawn lumber, on the other hand, incorporates two very distinct grain patterns. Toward the edge of a board, the grain is essentially quartersawn, with straight lines close together. In the center, there is a cathedral effect, which often reverses itself from one end of the board to the other. So, one might begin a cut with the grain and end it against the grain. Taking light cuts and changing the direction of the cut to match the direction of the grain both help.

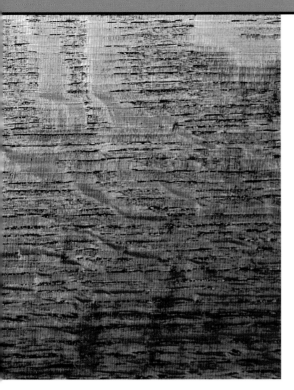

Carbide cutters

When it comes to carbide tips (usually tungsten carbide), clear answers about bevel angles are more difficult to get. The speed at which a carbide cutter sharpens on a diamond sharpener indicates how hard it is, and a cutter that takes longer to sharpen is harder than one that sharpens quickly. You don't get carbide tips on hand tools, only on machine cutters, which makes it possible for their bevels to be highly engineered. However, a bad sharpening can inadvertently change the angle of address, and this can be extremely detrimental to the quality of the cut. Carbide meets the work head-on, or nearly so, and it depends on hardness, power, and speed to shear rather than slice. Even a slight deviation administered by a questionable sharpening shop can do serious harm to the cutter's efficiency.

Carbide is graded on a scale ranging from C1 to C4, and a naive approach would be to assume C1 is for rough cutting, C4 is for fine cutting, and the other grades fit somewhere in between. That leads to the assumption C4 is "better," which is not at all true. C4 is definitely harder than C1 (about 93 on the Rockwell scale, compared with 90.5), and therefore, it's probably more brittle. Some carbide cutters are angled at almost 90 degrees to the axis of rotation for optimum performance, as shown in **Figure 9-6**, making the brittle material less likely to chip.

A virtual visit to the Website of Carbide Processors Inc. in Seattle will quickly dispel any illusions of a simple explanation of carbide grades. The company has published a free book online (*www. carbideprocessors. com/Brazing/book*) that covers everything a woodworker would ever want to know about carbide.

Hardwoods are more easily cut with a higher angle than softwoods. A pine log furniture builder might set the bevel of a plane at 25 degrees, while a cabinetmaker who uses a lot of hickory may prefer something in the neighborhood of 30 or even 35 degrees. Again, there is no substitute for experience...and experimenting.

The quality of the steel in a cutter is another vital consideration. Hard steel is brittle, will take a sharper edge, and will lose it more quickly than softer steel. Experimenting with the bevel begins with discovering the hardness of the steel. Asking the manufacturer is the best way to get an answer here. One could, theoretically, have the blade's hardness tested on a Rockwell tester, but that seems a little overboard. A more reasonable option is to begin with a lower bevel and experiment slowly, adding a couple of degrees until you achieve optimum performance. If the edge doesn't hold very long, retard it a couple of degrees and try again. Problems won't usually appear until angles are higher than 40 degrees. As the micro-bevel angle approaches 45 degrees, the heel of the bevel is going to contact the work and hold the sharp edge up in the air, where it can't cut anything.

Figure 9-6. Carbide is so hard and so brittle the geometry needs to be engineered for impact rather than slicing.

Figure 9-7. Paring chisels usually arrive with a 25-degree primary bevel and no secondary bevel, so they need to be honed before use, as shown in the inset photo.

Carving Tools

Carving tools are difficult to categorize. They are so specialized there really are no common rules. Unless the angle of the factory bevel is known, the best advice is to establish a 20-degree angle for softwoods and a 25-degree bevel for hardwoods and experiment from there.

Chisels

Straight chisels, also called paring chisels (see **Figure 9-7**), usually come with a primary bevel of about 25 degrees. Some come out of the box with a secondary bevel of 2 or 3 degrees, but most need to be honed to create the secondary bevel and to flatten the back face. If they are going to be used with a mallet, an extra 5 degrees is a good idea. The extra metal will help absorb the impact of a hammer or mallet blow. Mortising chisels should have a primary bevel in the 32-degree range.

Jointer Knives

Jointer knives usually ship with a 35-degree single bevel (no secondary), and many of them are disposable. That doesn't preclude a couple of light sharpenings, and there are tools made to do this without even removing the knives, as shown in **Figure 9-8**.

Recommended bevel angles

The next paragraphs list recommended angles for various cutters. Note that some of the tools have both a primary (large) bevel and a secondary (small) bevel, while others, such as lathe tools, have only a primary bevel. Lathe tools are sharpened often and don't require as fine an edge as, say, a mortising chisel. The given angles are a guide. The numbers are not critical, and each woodworker will change them a little as he or she experiments and gains experience. They are, however, a good starting point. And bear in mind the factory angle takes precedence over any recommendations made here, as a starting point for experimenting.

Axes

Axes sharpened on two faces come with a 15-degree bevel on each side, and axes sharpened on one face are generally shipped with a 23-degree bevel, or thereabouts.

Bench Planes

Bench planes typically have a 25- to 30-degree primary bevel, as do block planes. The tools have different pitches, and the bench plane iron is mounted bevel down while the block plane is bevel up, so even though they have the same bevel angle, they contact the work at different angles, and in a different manner.

Figure 9-8. One doesn't have to remove jointer knives from the machine to give them a quick honing with this little jig.

Router Bits

Anybody sharpening router bits should try to maintain or revert to the angle set at the factory. A trip to the hardware store will usually reveal what that was because bits don't seem to change once a style or size has been established. High-speed steel (HSS) bits almost always have more acute angles than carbide-tipped bits.

Turning Tools

Angles on turning tools are very subjective. Because of the mixed, exotic, and figured woods often used in turning, almost every project requires individual consideration. Lathe speed is an issue, too. Some lathe tools arrive with no bevel at all, while others are designed by individual turners, custom built, and created to do very specific tasks. Even the height of the lathe tool rest and the turner play a role. Many lathe tools scrape rather than cut, and the angles are far larger (about 75 degrees).

In general, lathe tools have higher bevel angles than bench tools. If they were as acute, they would not be able to withstand the constant impact of a spinning workpiece. Standard lathe chisels usually have a 45-degree factory bevel, which gets smaller with the turner's experience. Over the years, one learns to shear rather than scrape, and the tendency is to work toward a bevel in the 35-degree range.

A skew has two beveled faces and an angle across the leading edge. A good starting spot for that angle is 30 degrees. If the tool will be cutting a lot of convex and concave profiles, consider leaving an arc on the trailing edge rather than grinding it as a straight line, as shown in **Figure 9-9**. There also is a school of thought that says the arc itself should be concave instead of convex. Many discussion forums on the Internet feature arguments for both concepts. (This is one of those exquisite areas of woodworking where a whole day can be spent learning almost nothing except how to avoid household chores.) The bevels on the two faces of a skew should each be 11 degrees. For fine work, hard stock, and slower speeds, a 13-degree angle may work better, but start at the lower angle.

A roughing gouge is bigger and longer than a spindle gouge and is used to core (that is, round a blank to a cylindrical shape between centers) or else to remove a large amount of waste in a short time. Most lathe starter sets include a spindle gouge and no roughing gouge. A roughing gouge should be ground straight across, with a 45-degree bevel applied to the trailing edge. Roughing gouges are usually touched up on the grindstone, and some people like to remove the burr from the trailing edge with a slip stone or with fine sandpaper rolled on a dowel. They are rarely honed. However, stropping or buffing can help.

Spindle and bowl gouges are smaller and narrower than roughing gouges, and their ends can vary from straight across to a completely round arc and beyond. In general, spindle gouges have a smaller arc than deep bowl gouges. The more extreme (long) the arc is, the more the sides of it can be used to scrape while the front cuts. The back bevel on most spindle gouges begins around 40 to 45 degrees.

Figure 9-9. Turners handling lots of convex and concave profiles might enjoy experimenting with the shape of their skew.

Back bevels

A back bevel is a small bevel (up to 12 degrees or so) ground on the flat back face of a cutter. Experienced woodworkers will often grind such a bevel on plane irons, jointer knives, and other wide cutters, as shown in **Figure 9-10**. The idea is the point of the blade can be ground and honed to a highly effective 38 degrees or so (for example, a 25-degree primary, a 3-degree secondary, and a 10-degree back bevel). Such practice can pay large dividends on highly figured wood, where the cutter can slice or scrape through grain coming at it in several directions.

For the vast majority of tasks, however, a back bevel is not a great idea. Honing to such an extreme angle has two consequences. First, it requires constant maintenance because the edge, being asked to scrape as much as it slices, breaks down more quickly than usual. And second, it requires having more than one iron for the plane in question or more than one set of jointer knives because once you do add the back bevel, you won't want to regrind to get rid of it.

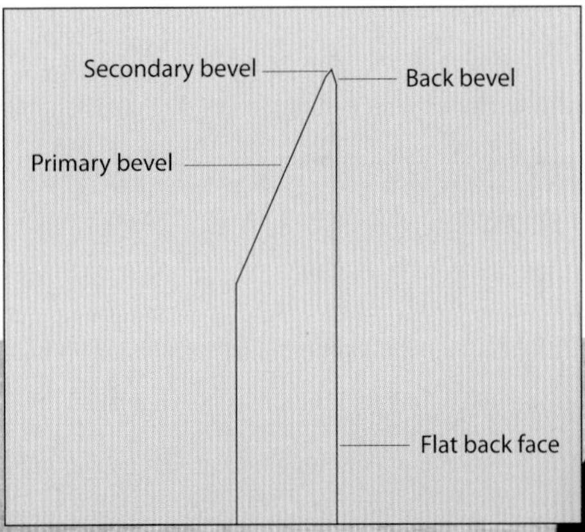

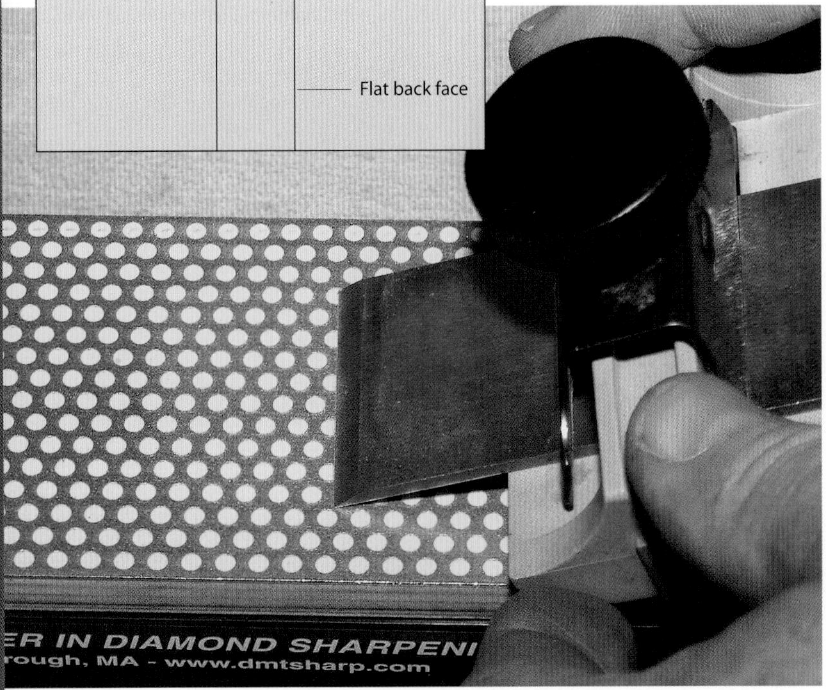

Most back bevels are actually in the smaller range (around 5 degrees) and are honed rather than ground. The quality of steel can be a major factor in the success of a back bevel, too. Brittle, hard steel has a greater chance of breaking down when used on difficult wood.

If one wishes to reverse the effect of a back bevel, the cutter needs to be reground all the way through the bevel, and a new primary bevel must be established on the leading edge. So, for woodworkers who decide to go that route and create a back bevel on their tools, a second set of irons or knives is a sound investment. If your work favors hand tools, extra plane irons are a good idea anyway since you can just swap a sharp one for a dull one without interrupting your work for a sharpening session.

The magic of jigs

Deciding on a bevel angle is a matter of judgment. Establishing the angle is usually done with a gauge or guide. Once the bevel angle has been set, a jig is the simplest way to maintain it while grinding or honing.

Most bench stone and grinder suppliers recommend some form of jig to keep the blade at a specific angle while sharpening. The concept behind jigs is the angle of a hand-held blade will change almost every time the operator moves, shifts weight from one foot to another, gets tired hands, stops and starts sharpening, and so on. A jig, on the other hand, always holds the blade at a specific angle. One can sharpen, use the tool, and come back to the jig to resharpen, and the angle of address won't move a micron. That kind of consistency, reliability, and repeatability is the heart of sharpening. Another advantage to using jigs is one can establish a constant (say, 25 degrees), and while experimenting, deviate from that constant. If the experiment is less than satisfactory, regrinding to the original angle is not a problem.

Figure 9-10. A small back bevel can improve performance in difficult grain, but it takes quite a bit of grinding to remove.

Secondary bevel

Back bevel

Primary bevel

Flat back face

ER IN DIAMOND SHARPENI
rough, MA - www.dmtsharp.com

Jigs range from very simple shop-built affairs to some highly technical commercial solutions. Most are adjustable in one way or another and are relatively inexpensive considering the amount of time and effort they save. They generally fall into two categories, grinding jigs and honing jigs. The following is a brief survey of some popular jigs. The summary is by no means exhaustive because jigs change constantly.

Burns Jig

Furniture and guitar builder Brian Burns of Fort Bragg, California, has designed one of the most successful honing jigs on the market, shown in **Figure 9-11**. Perhaps "jig" is the wrong word here, because it's more than a mere jig. Over 20-some years and numerous tweaks, Burns has developed a complete system that has a very strong following among professional woodworkers. The package includes a small book entitled *Double Bevel Sharpening*, plus a sharpening stone box and the actual bevel guide. Available through such reputable sources as The Japan Woodworker and similar retailers, the system is well worth a look for luthiers and anybody else who is working with figured woods and low tolerances. The essence of the double-bevel theory is that back bevels (see page 62) can dramatically improve results in both hard and figured grain patterns.

Figure 9-11. Tired of using lesser jigs, luthier Brian Burns designed this jig to hone planes for his guitar-making business.

Japanese Planes and Chisels

The iron in a Japanese plane is radically different from, and quite a bit harder than, Western irons (about five points on the Rockwell scale). Designed to be pulled rather than pushed, such planes can remove a very thin shaving. However, they do require knowledge and experience to get it right. The pulling action is not as controlled in novice hands as a Western push, and it's hard to lean into the plane to ensure complete contact with the work. Once mastered, however, Japanese planes are a joy to use. Japanese chisels are also harder than Western ones.

Japanese plane irons and chisels (see **Figure 9-12**) shouldn't be hollow ground, because they are laminated (see Grinding Hollow or Flat on pages 74-75). A very hard cutting edge (the hagane, a white steel) is layered onto a bed of soft steel or iron (the jigane), and hollow grinding would reduce the amount of support offered by the softer material. The blades also have a small hollow in the back.

The advantage of a hollow back is there is less material to hone, but it means Japanese blades need to be tuned occasionally. That involves hammering out the back to provide a flat edge for sharpening. Several Websites offer hammers for this task, and plenty of advice, too.

The best way to sharpen Japanese planes and chisels is on Japanese water stones, with a bevel of 30 degrees for softwoods and 35 degrees for hardwoods, working down through the grits to 8000. The Shapton ceramic system is a good option, too. Shapton has polishing stones up to 30,000-grit, which will produce the finest edge a Japanese chisel or plane can hold. The steel should be dried when done, and lightly oiled if the tool won't be used soon.

Figure 9-12. On Japanese chisels, a hard-cutting edge is laminated to a bed of soft steel, so they aren't hollow ground.

DMT Aligner

Most jigs are specialized, meaning they are intended for sharpening knives, turning tools, or flat bench tools. The Aligner from Diamond Machining Technology is a perfect example of a specialized jig. The compact honing jig is very effective when used with knives that don't have serrated edges, as shown in **Figure 9-13**. Designed for use with 4" (110 mm) diamond whetstones, it is very flexible, has seven presets for holding knives at different angles during honing, and can be adapted for use with other stones.

General Tools

An old favorite with woodworkers is the 809 jig from General Tools, shown in **Figure 9-14**. Its high-impact, fiberglass-reinforced Lexan body folds almost flat for storage, and a steel clamp holds the cutter in place. The 809 has graduated settings designed to maintain a 30-degree cutting angle on chisels or plane blades, but it can comfortably be adjusted by at least 20 degrees in either direction. The friction lock on the hinge

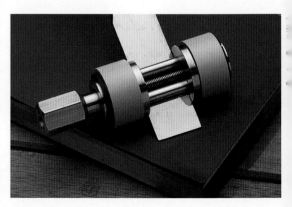

Figure 9-14. An old favorite with woodworkers is the 809 honing jig from General Tools, which is large and comfortable to use.

is very reliable. Embossed settings on the hinge are for 2"-, 1½"-, 1"-, and ½"-thick stones and diamond sharpeners, and the jig adjusts all the way down to zero inches for sandpaper or to an array of angles that will accommodate just about any bevel. The spring-loaded clamp handles blades up to 2⅝" wide.

Kell Jig

An attractive choice is the British-made, two-wheel drive Kell No.1 honing guide, shown in **Figure 9-15**. Beautifully engineered for a lifetime of use, the jig is ideally suited to bench and mortising chisels. It has two solid, turned-brass bobbins, each fitted with a Delrin roller, which run on stainless steel guide rods. A threaded rod through the center is used to tighten the bobbins to the side of a chisel, using a solid brass

Figure 9-13. The Aligner from DMT has seven presets for holding various tools at different angles during honing.

Figure 9-15. This exquisitely engineered honing jig is built one at a time in England by master craftsman Richard Kell.

Bench Stones 1: Ergonomics: The Technique of Sharpening

The traditional Japanese method of using water stones involves a very low bench or squatting over the stone so one's own mass becomes part of the equation. Here in the West, we prefer to stand. We also use jigs and machines, so we are perhaps less in tune with the process, even though we have more control of its elements.

Ideally, a person's center of gravity should be as close as possible to the center of the work when using bench stones (see **Figure 1**), and the eyes should be able to follow the action through the complete stroke. To that end, Norm Abram has a pull-out step in his sharpening center, which elevates him above the work (see **Figure 2**). (For more on Norm Abram's sharpening center, see page 134.)

The technique of sharpening with a bench stone requires some practice and attention to detail. With the tool locked in a jig, press down toward the front of the blade (see **Figure 3**), and steer with the back of the jig. Press hard enough to hear and feel the rich sensation of the stone cutting steel, but not so hard that the cutter might slip and gouge the stone. Keep the work wet on oilstones and water stones (diamonds work well wet or dry), and use the direction of strokes to spread the swarf evenly around the stone (see **Figure 4**). This visually helps to reduce uneven wear.

Check occasionally with a try square to make sure the edge is at right angles to the long sides. Most of the cutting action occurs on the forward stroke, so apply pressure accordingly. Pressing too hard on the backstroke can lead to a lessening of control. Right-handed people usually feel more comfortable standing to the left of a stone, and vise versa.

A stone must not be able to move on the bench. A simple jig can be built using a cutoff of solid surface material, a small block of hardwood, and some lightweight brass sheet stock. Bend the brass about 80 degrees, and it will act as a spring to lightly lock the stone in place (see **Figure 5**). A few strips of skateboard tape on the bottom will prevent slipping along the bench (see **Figure 6**).

Figure 1. The sharpener's center of gravity should be over the work, or close to it.

Figure 2. A pull-out step on this sharpening station helps the sharpener get on top of the work.

Figure 3. With the tool locked in a jig, press down on the front with one hand and steer from the back with the other.

Figure 4. Spread the swarf all around on the surface of the stone.

Figure 5. A block of wood and a bent brass strip traps the stone on a solid surface material board.

Figure 6. Skateboard tape keeps this sharpening board from sliding around on the bench.

Figure 9-16. Kell's largest honing jig works beautifully for skew chisels, which are held in place with a wooden wedge.

knob. The chisel can be secured under the guide bars, or above them, making it possible to accurately hone very short or very narrow chisels, or chisels with extremely long primary bevels.

While the No.1 guide is designed primarily for chisels that are from ⅟₃₂" to 1⅛" wide (Kell specifies nominal dimensions of 0" to 1"), a larger version, the Kell No. 2, handles chisels and plane irons up to 2⅝" wide. And for skews, Kell has designed another jig, the Number 3, shown in **Figure 9-16**, which has large self-lubricating rollers that are very broadly spaced, with pins to locate the chisel. The jig uses a wooden wedge to secure the skew, and it comes with plans to make that simple wedge.

Aesthetically delightful, hand-made jigs such as these sometimes find their way out of the workshop and onto the corner of one's desk, or perhaps onto a library shelf—which would be a shame since the jig really does work well. The exquisite machining is reminiscent of an earlier time when British craftsmanship traveled an empire. All three jigs are available in the United States through such reputable suppliers as Garrett Wade and Hartville Tools.

No-Name Jig

A jig that is widely available in home centers but which bears no maker's stamp (see **Figure 9-17**) is not impressive. Running on a single narrow wheel, its geometry seems clumsy, unstable, and poorly balanced—and in shop tests, it did not deliver the kind of results one might desire.

Figure 9-17. Some honing jigs have narrow wheels, poor geometry, and rough casting, which makes them not worth their price.

Pinnacle Honing Guide

The Pinnacle honing guide (see **Figure 9-18**) is a sophisticated jig from Woodcraft Supply that offers a high degree of repeatability, and it works with all kinds of bench stones, wet/dry sandpaper, and even diamond paste. It also works well with the new honing films from Woodcraft (see below). Because the sled holds the tool in a fixed relationship to the abrasive surface, it's pretty much impossible to sharpen past a set angle. According to the company, the sled "provides a stable platform, virtually eliminating any side-to-side roll."

The way it works is a sled rides on a couple of rails while holding the tool at the correct angle and depth. The jig has six primary positive stops at 15 degrees, 20 degrees, 25 degrees, 30 degrees, 35 degrees, and 40 degrees, as well as six corresponding micro-bevel positions from 17 degrees through 42 degrees. The sled can be used alone on any smooth, flat surface, such as a granite stone or glass lapping plate, or with the rails and a bench stone that measures up to 3" x 11½". The kit includes the honing guide, honing plate, and a honing film assortment pack. The film has a micro-fine, high-grade grit, and each pack includes three 8" x 2⅝" abrasive sheets. The film is adhesive-backed, or it can be applied to an impervious flat surface with soap and water for easy removal and reuse. Grits include 15 micron, 5 micron, and 0.3 micron.

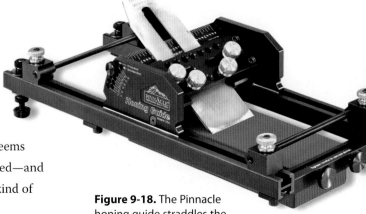

Figure 9-18. The Pinnacle honing guide straddles the sharpening stone with a sled that carries the tool-holding jig.

Bench Stones 2: The Sequence of Sharpening

The first step in using stones is to make sure they are flat. Water stones can be flattened with other water stones, with diamond stones (see **Figure 1**), or with wet/dry paper on a lapping plate. Commercial flattening stones are available, too. Oilstones don't wear nearly as much as water stones (and they work slower), but they still need an occasional flattening. Use the same method, but set aside some extra time because oilstones are hard and dense.

When working with chisels and plane irons, flatten the backs first (see **Figure 2**). Keep in mind you only have to flatten an inch or so up the blade (see **Figure 3**), not the whole back face. Flattening should only need to be done when a tool is new, has been damaged, or has been subjected to extremes of heat and cold (which may cause warping). Work down through the grits, moving on when all of the scratches made by the previous grit have disappeared. Keep the surface wet with oil or water, depending on the type of stone. If the stone goes dry, it may glaze and need to be lapped again. Make one final pass with each grit, traveling at a slightly different angle to the rest so the scratches are more visible (see **Figure 4**). Doing so shows you what needs to be removed in the next step and also highlights any slight hollows that might otherwise be missed. Clean up after using each grit because coarse swarf will make a coarse stone out of a fine one.

When the back is perfectly flat, it's time to tackle the front (beveled) side of the blade. Follow the same sequence, keeping in mind honing only works the small secondary bevel, so it requires a lot less work. Here, scratches are more difficult to see, so a magnifying glass or a jeweler's loupe is a real boon (see **Figure 5**). Feel intermittently with your fingertips for the tiny burr, a coarse ridge on the back of the blade, that is being raised. When it extends all the way across the edge, it's time to move to the next finest grit. Remove the final burr by stropping or buffing with a charged wheel (see **Figure 6**).

Figure 1. Flatten sharpening stones with a diamond stone or plate.

Figure 2. Flatten the back face of chisels and plane irons.

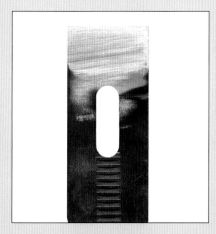

Figure 3. Flatten the leading inch or so of the back, not the entire surface.

Figure 4. Make the last strokes at an angle to make any scratches more visible.

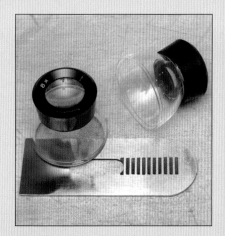

Figure 5. A close look at the edge is a big help.

Figure 6. Remove the burr on a fine bench stone or by stropping on a charged wheel.

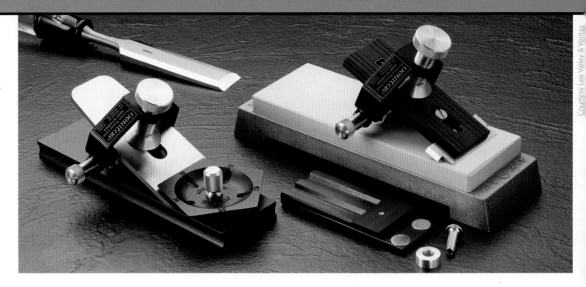

Figure 9-19. The Veritas honing system uses a pentagonal gauge to set the angle at which the tool is locked in the jig.

Shapton

One company that does not offer a jig to go with its sharpening system is Shapton. Instead, Shapton supplies a video that teaches one how to stand and how to hold the tool freehand during sharpening.

Veritas

The system by Veritas uses a pentagonal gauge to set the angle for a honing jig, shown in **Figure 9-19** with a plane iron installed. The jig then locks the tool to be sharpened at that angle, using a knurled brass knob. It holds cutters up to 2⅜"-wide. If the tool is too short for the jig, a spokeshave blade for example, Veritas offers a special holder to extend its length. A bigger version of the honing guide, the Mark II, shown in **Figure 9-20**, holds irons and blades as wide as 2⅞" and has three positive stops for different angles. Also shown is the Veritas registration jig, which is used to align and square the blade in the honing guide.

Figure 9-20. The Veritas registration jig is used to align and square the blade in the honing guide.

Specialty jigs

There are a number of interesting and useful specialty jigs for particular categories of tools such as cabinet scrapers and drill bits. While experienced workers are likely to sharpen these tools freehand, most would find one of the jigs a real help. Drill bits in particular are not likely to remain symmetrical in freehand sharpening, and they won't work very well when they are not symmetrical, so a jig is a big help.

Cabinet Scrapers

One specialty jig worth mentioning is a clamp from the Woodsmith Store (see **Figure 9-21**) that allows you to file a perfect edge on cabinet scrapers. The jig also has an attached burnishing pin.

Figure 9-21. This patented jig from Woodsmith uses a file to put a perfect edge on the straight sides of cabinet scrapers.

Figure 9-22. Some jigs use other tools to sharpen, such as this clamp that holds a portable drill steady for stropping.

Drill Mount

Some jigs borrow power from electric drills to provide a quick and simple solution for woodworkers on a job site, where proper sharpening solutions are not available. One such device, the Switch 'N Lock Drill Mount (available from suppliers such as Rockler Woodworking and Hardware), works well with a leather wheel strop, especially with a variable-speed drill (**Figure 9-22**).

General Tools

General Tools also makes the #825 drill bit sharpener, shown in **Figure 9-23**. The inexpensive device works with virtually any grindstone and has presets at all the most common twist bit angles (176 degrees, 136 degrees, 118 degrees, and 98 degrees). It can handle shafts from ⅛" to ¾" in diameter, and it is surprisingly effective, although it does beg a word of caution: Drill bits sharpened on 3,450 rpm (standard speed) grinders are very susceptible to overheating. A slow-speed grinder is highly recommended, and a reservoir of cold water is essential to keep the bit cool. An identical version of the jig is available from Homier.

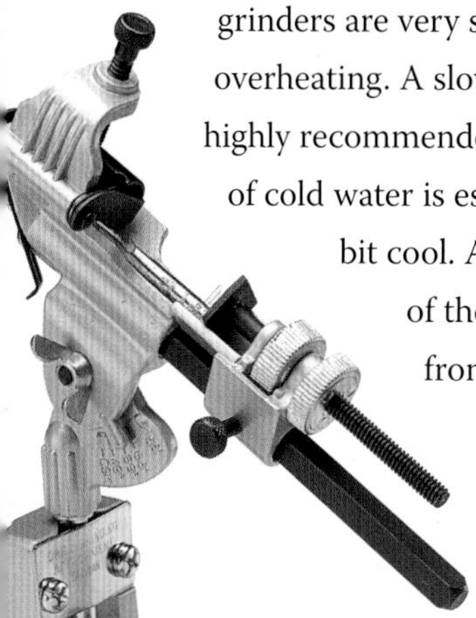

Figure 9-23. Used with a standard bench grinder, the jig holds high-speed steel drill bits at the correct angle for sharpening.

Turning tool jigs

Nobody sharpens as frequently as a turner. Even carvers and whittlers, who have an incessant need to strop and hone, spend less time than woodturners in search of a perfect edge. The reason, of course, is constant contact with a spinning workpiece, which abrades and wears down an edge in the blink of an eye. Turners mostly grind their tools and go straight to the lathe with the ground edge.

Figure 9-24. An elegantly simple jig from an elegant craftsman, Ellsworth's jig comes with a great deal of information.

Ellsworth Jig

A simple jig for turners, the Ellsworth Jig (see **Figure 9-24**), was designed by noted turner David Ellsworth of Quakertown, Pennsylvania. Created to maintain the characteristic tip shape of Ellsworth's "Signature" gouge, the jig works on any size of grinding wheel from 6" to 8 ". It comes with instructions on how to make and set up the sliding arm (not included), plus illustrations on what the shape looks like and how to correct problems. Ellsworth recommends "using gouges with a parabolic flute shape in the diameters of ½", ⅝", and the new 16.5 mm powder metal (Pro PM). The jig is fabricated in aluminum and has a floating cap on the setscrew that will not mushroom and slip on the tool shaft. It will work with a shop-made sliding arm (shown), although one can also use a Wolverine sliding arm or the 'Vertical Solution' made by Don Geiger specifically for (this) jig."

Oneway Wolverine

Among the most highly regarded jigs for turning tools is the Wolverine from Oneway Manufacturing (see

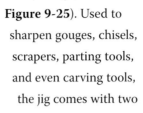

Figure 9-25). Used to sharpen gouges, chisels, scrapers, parting tools, and even carving tools, the jig comes with two bases because grinders come with two wheels. Both bases are equipped with cam-lock clamping for the quick switching of tools. The adjustable angle platform has a three-inch-by-five-inch worktop that can be used on both the left- and right-hand sides of the grinder.

One part of the Wolverine system worth noting is a jig named the Vari-Grind (see **Figure 9-26**), which is designed to help shape and maintain the edge on standard bowl gouges. According to Oneway, it also works for "the modern side grind (also known as the Ellsworth grind, Liam O'Neil grind, or Irish grind) and the traditional fingernail shape for spindlework detailing."

Sorby Fingernail Grinder

The Sorby Fingernail Grinder from Lee Valley (see **Figure 9-27**) is a similar type of jig to the Ellsworth, and it too is worth a look. It comes factory set to replicate a medium (60 degrees) fingernail profile and takes up a lot less space.

Figure 9-25. The Wolverine jig is designed for turning tools and features an adjustable arm that establishes the bevel angle.

Figure 9-26. The Vari-Grind jig holds turning gouges and controls their movement in an elliptical pattern for a fingernail grind.

Figure 9-27. Short and to the point, the Sorby jig takes up very little bench space and uses an XYZ clamp for gouges.

Woodcut Tru-Grind

Similar in some respects to the Wolverine system, the Tru-Grind jig from Woodcut Tools Limited in New Zealand (see **Figure 9-28**) can sharpen a huge range of turning, carving, and carpenter's tools, bits, drills, and many other items. It fits most bench grinders and comes with an instructional video.

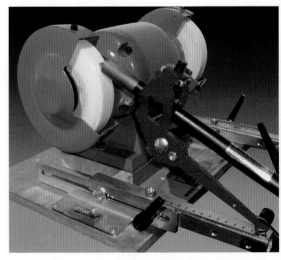

Figure 9-29. The Tru-Grind from Woodcut Tools of New Zealand sharpens turning, carving, and carpentry tools.

Bench Stones 3: Different Stones, Different Techniques

Oilstones, water stones, sandpaper lapping plates, and diamond bench stones all share a common methodology, but there are some succinct differences among them. The first thing to keep in mind is the height of the stone. When setting a bevel jig, the wheel should ideally be running on a surface at the same height as the top of the stone, if not actually on the stone (see **Figure 1**). For some jigs, it's a good idea to have some plywood plates available to build up a small area of the tabletop to the right height. Some jigs have readings built in for various thicknesses of stones (see **Figure 2**).

Liquids on bench stones are cleaners, not lubricants. One doesn't actually want to lubricate the process— the basic concept is to create friction, not eliminate it. The function of water and oil is to move waste out of the way so it doesn't become forced into pores in the stone and create a glaze. Water can be used on all four options (including oilstones), but oil must never, ever be used on water stones or ceramic stones. It will immediately clog most stones, although it can be used in a pinch on diamonds. The coarser an oilstone is, the more oil it requires to charge it.

Diamonds are the most aggressive sharpeners (see **Figure 3**), followed by water stones, and then oilstones. In the early and middle stages of sharpening (where coarse and medium grits are used), diamonds are quite effective and remarkably quick (**Figure 4**). As one reaches very fine grits, oilstones and water stones can ultimately deliver a cleaner edge. There is a point of diminishing returns, however, where the chisel or plane is sharp enough to do its job (see **Figure 5**) and creating an even finer edge won't elevate the visible quality of the work. Also, an extremely fine edge will break down faster than a very fine one. That reality is a logical argument for staying with diamond stones down to 7 microns or 9 microns and stopping there, especially with turning and carving tools (see **Figure 6**). For example, a diamond slip works very quickly to remove the burr from the inside of a gouge.

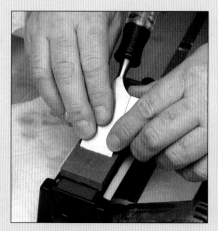

Figure 1. When setting a bevel jig, its wheel should run on the stone or on a surface at the same height.

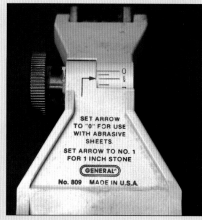

Figure 2. Some bevel jigs have built-in readings to match the stone's thickness.

Figure 3. Diamonds are the most aggressive sharpeners.

Figure 4. Diamond stones are remarkably quick in the early and middle stages of sharpening.

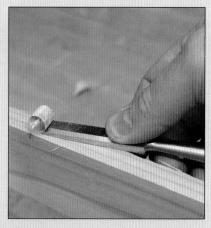

Figure 5. A tool is sharp enough when it does its job well, and further sharpening won't actually improve it.

Figure 6. A diamond slip removes the burr from the inside of this carving gouge.

CHAPTER 10

Sharpening Machines

Tackling the tedium of sharpening, dedicated machines offer speed and control. The key is having the stone move rather than the tool. However, there's a lot to be said for learning how to sharpen manually before stepping up to a dedicated machine. It's all about feeling and degree. The object of sharpening is to produce a keen edge while removing as little of the tool as possible. The temptation with machines is to remove too much steel, simply because it doesn't require a lot of work.

Sharpening machines can do three things, depending on how they are set up. They can grind, hone, or strop/buff. In Chapter 10, I'll discuss the alternatives; then, I'll review the various sharpening machines you can buy, from the simplest to the most complex.

Grinding hollow or flat

Some sharpening machines are designed to grind a flat bevel, while others grind a hollow bevel, as shown in **Figure 10-1**. A hollow bevel is one where the main bevel has been formed by holding the tool (chisel, plane knife, etc.) against the edge of a vertically mounted round wheel. The result is a hollow, concave surface. If the bevel were formed on the side of the same wheel, or on a flat bench stone, the result would be a flat bevel.

There are arguments in favor of and against both types of bevel, but the bottom line is that, for most woodworkers, it doesn't make a whole lot of difference. The secondary, small bevel at the tip of a cutter is far more critical than the large, primary bevel—and usually, that secondary one is so small (perhaps ¹⁄₁₆" wide at most) that the difference between a hollow and a flat profile would hardly be noticeable. There is an argument that hollow grinds are not quite as strong as flat ones, which is an exaggeration unless the wheel (grindstone) is very small and it produces a dramatic hollow.

Some experts would suggest that on a vertical-wheel machine, buying the largest-diameter wheel possible is a good idea because it will produce a less severe hollow bevel than a smaller wheel. In fact, some old hand-

operated grindstones found on farms across the country measured up to two feet in diameter. However, today a wheel of eight inches or more in diameter is a good choice. The ten-inch stone on a Tormek sharpening machine pretty much eliminates any argument about wheel diameter, but some bench grinders do come with wheels as small as five inches. When the wheel is small, altering the angle of address can minimize the hollow. For example, if the tool is presented to the wheel at a 20-degree angle, the hollow will be shorter than the same tool being presented at 25 degrees (see Chapter 9: Angles and Jigs for a discussion on angles).

Many machines don't use the edge of the wheel to grind, like a vertical stone does in order to create a hollow bevel. Instead, the wheel is turned 90 degrees (that is, the stone is laid on its side), and the horizontal sides are used to deliver a flat bevel, as shown in **Figure 10-2**. On slow water-cooled wheels, it introduces a design variation. Instead of the bottom of a vertical wheel being continually immersed in a water bath as it rotates, water has to be introduced to a horizontal stone from above. A second, and perhaps more telling, difference is machines using a horizontal stone have a differential inequality. Different parts of the stone travel at different speeds. Each time an 8" stone rotates, a spot located 2" from the center travels about 7", while a spot near the edge travels about 2'.

That differential means the stone wears at different rates across its surface. Dressing a horizontal stone (making it flat) used to be more difficult than doing the same to a vertical stone. Now, we can just lay a diamond sharpener across it, turn on the machine, and in seconds the stone is dressed, as shown in **Figure 10-3**.

Horizontal stones generally offer a wider abrasive surface, making it easier to sharpen wide knives. The Tormek system addresses it by using a wheel up to 2" wide, depending on the model. Most bench grinders employ a ¾"-thick wheel.

Figure 10-1. Tools ground on the edge of a wheel have a hollow grind (bottom), while those ground on the flat side of a wheel or on a bench stone have a flat grind (top).

Figure 10-2. On fast vertical wheels (inset), the edge is used to grind, while slow horizontal wheels use the side.

Figure 10-3. Diamond hones are an ideal way to level and dress a slow horizontal wheel, and they work better without water.

A horizontal stone also offers a gravitational advantage when it comes to creating swarf, which reuses metal and stone waste to help polish the edge being formed. It can be hard to maintain swarf on a vertical grinder, especially one with a narrow edge that is continually immersed in a bath of water and washed clean.

Dry grinders

Bench grinders were developed more than 70 years ago to take advantage of advances in electrical motors. Most of these motors rotate at either 1,725 or 3,450 rpm. The one shown in **Figure 10-4**, which woodworker Chris Billman photographed in his own shop, runs at the slower speed. It generates a lot less heat than the faster version. Grindstones are direct drive, which is known in the industry as being "motorized." There are no belts and pulleys, so the stone rotates at the same speed as the motor. That's a very high rate of speed, which quickly builds up heat in the steel being ground. This is why many novices destroy tools when they first attempt to sharpen them. By the time a piece of steel turns visibly red or blue, it has already gone through several less visible color changes related to a buildup of heat. It was damaged long before the tip went blue (**Figure 10-5**). What happens is the temper of the metal is changed by intense heat, and it becomes too brittle to hold a sharp edge. Grinding on a dry stone takes skill.

Carbon steel will lose its temper at a lower temperature than high-speed steel (something in the neighborhood of 600°F and 1,000°F respectively, depending on the carbon content). Both will begin to visibly discolor at about 500°. The best choice is to never get the tool so hot you can't handle it. That means frequently dipping it in cool water, putting it on the grindstone with very little pressure, and touching it against the wheel for just a few seconds at a time.

Some metalworkers will tell you dipping the tool in water is a bad idea because it can shock the steel. It is a process similar to "springing" a saucepan by removing it from the stove and immersing it in cold water right away. A pan so treated can lose its shape. However, if a tool never gets too hot to handle, it's hard to see how it could be shocked. It can rust, of course, so always dry the tool after dipping.

A favorite among woodturners, bench grinders are quick and aggressive, and do just the trick when thrusting tools into spinning wood. It doesn't make sense to continually hone and strop to an ultra-fine edge when it will only last a few seconds on a lathe. A huge part of turning is removing large volumes of waste wood, and a ground edge is certainly fine enough for this task. Most turners will hone only before they get to the refining stage. Master turner Alan Lacer likes to hone with a dry oilstone slip, while Ellis Hein likes to grind and then strop with a charged paper wheel. One huge advantage to the lathe is a very fine surface can be achieved with abrasive papers while the workpiece is spinning, obviating the need to hone scrapers to achieve a silky finish.

Photo by Chris Billman

Figure 10-4. For sharpeners who choose to use a standard grinder, an 8" slow-speed (1,725 rpm) machine is an excellent choice.

Photo by author, permission of woodworker.com

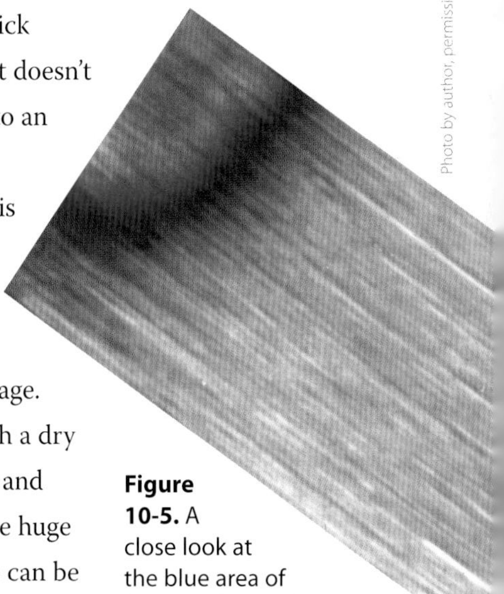

Figure 10-5. A close look at the blue area of this chisel reveals a sequential array of colors related to overheating the steel.

Choosing a dry grinder

A good-quality 1,725 rpm grinder is the best choice. Most commercially available grinders run at 3,450 rpm, which is really quite fast and generates a lot of heat. An 8" wheel is perfect because it won't reveal a deep hollow (that is, it makes a shallow hollow grind). Delta and Baldor both make excellent 1,750 rpm dry grinders that accept 8" wheels.

Figure 10-6. Grinders work well with friable wheels in the J or K hardness range, and a buffing wheel is a sensible addition.

When using a grinder, sharpening should always begin with balanced wheels and trued stones. It's a good idea to replace the cheap grinding wheels supplied by some factories with friable aluminum oxide wheels, which are blue, white, or pink (see **Figure 10-6**). The coarse wheel should be 36-grit to 60-grit, and the fine wheel should be 80-grit to 100-grit. Look for a J or a K in the code stamped on the wheel, an ideal hardness for tool steel. For the more patient among us, a medium to fine wheel on one side and a buffing wheel (either shaped or flat) on the other can be a sensible option.

Before mounting a new wheel, you should draw a thin black pencil line across the outside face, with the line passing through the very center of the wheel. The line will come in handy when locking the platform or tool rest at specific angles by giving you a reference point.

Here are details on some dry grinders and grinding systems available on the U.S. market.

Delta

The Delta 23-725, shown in **Figure 10-7**, is an 8" industrial grade slow-speed grinder with a ¾ hp motor. It is an excellent choice for woodworkers who are wary of hollow grinds and would prefer to create a primary bevel on an 8" wheel. It comes with a flexible lamp, spark guards, eye shields, tool rests, a wheel dresser, an assembly wrench, two friable aluminum oxide wheels, a water tray, and an instruction manual. The wheels rotate at 1,725 rpm, which is half the speed of a standard bench grinder, but is still mighty fast. The 23-725 weighs in at a substantial 100 pounds, so there is no discernable vibration.

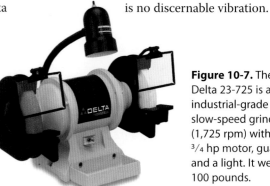

Figure 10-7. The Delta 23-725 is an 8" industrial-grade slow-speed grinder (1,725 rpm) with a ¾ hp motor, guards, and a light. It weighs 100 pounds.

Courtesy Delta Machinery

Grizzly Universal Knife Grinder

A dedicated machine designed to sharpen planer and jointer knives, the Grizzly G2790 (see **Figure 10-8**), is a dry grinder. According to the company, it has high-quality cast-iron construction and a large capacity (it will sharpen planer blades up to 20" wide). The heavy-duty motor is ½ hp with capacitor start, lubricated ball bearings, and a speed of 3,450 rpm. The knife holder angle adjusts from 15 degrees to 90 degrees, and the 120-grit stone raises and lowers as needed. With a half-inch arbor and a shipping weight of 58 pounds, the Grizzly G2790 is a serious machine for a dedicated purpose.

Figure 10-8. Grizzly's G2790 dry grinder has a large capacity (planer knives up to 20 inches wide) and a heavy-duty ½ hp motor.

Courtesy Grizzly Industrial, Inc.

GRS Power Hone

The GRS Power Hone (see **Figure 10-9**) uses diamond wheels to sharpen hardened steel, high-speed steel, and carbides. Designed for the engraving industry, it's worth a look by woodworkers, turners, and carvers. The wheels last for years and stay flat for accuracy, and different grits are available, from coarse to mirror polishing. With a heavy steel housing, continuous-duty motor, and double-bearing spindle, the GRS Power Hone is built to last and is remarkably easy to use. Although it is not a wet/dry system, the diamond wheel hones without building up heat, as a bench grinder would. The machine comes in 115-volt and 230-volt options, with a 600-grit diamond abrasive wheel. Videotaped, step-by-step instructions are available.

Figure 10-9. The GRS Power Hone uses a range of diamond wheels to sharpen hardened steel, high-speed steel, and carbides.

Sherwood Bench Grinder

Australia's Timbecon company began in May 1989 as a small retail outlet in Perth and has grown into one of Australia's leading woodworking tools suppliers. Timbecon's Sherwood bench grinder (MDN-200-E) (see **Figure 10-10**) features two 8"-diameter wheels and includes safety guards and rests.

Courtesy Timbecon

Figure 10-10. The Sherwood bench grinder from Timbecon has two dry 8" wheels.

Sherwood/Timbecon System

This high-quality system from Australia's Timbecon Pty Ltd. (see **Figure 10-11**) includes several jigs designed for general woodworking and turning. The Sherwood YF-6 grinder uses a slow, 6" horizontally-mounted, dry aluminum oxide wheel that is powered by a ½-hp motor. Various attachments are available, including the YFA-24 for knives up to 24" wide, the YFASM for chisels and plane irons, the DSA for sharpening twist drill bits, and a holder for a diamond dressing stone. The machine comes with a 100-grit stone, and a 320-grit fine stone is available.

Figure 10-11. The Sherwood machine from Timbecon offers several industrial-grade attachments for various sharpening tasks.

Veritas

The Veritas Mark II dry power sharpening system from Lee Valley (see **Figure 10-12**) is easy to use and delivers very satisfactory results. Spinning at 650 rpm, there is an intuitive feel to this machine that encourages freehand sharpening. Extra tool rests are available, so several tools can be set up simultaneously and sharpened on each grit. The large 8"-diameter aluminum plate on top of the machine takes adhesive-backed disks from 80-grit to 1,200-grit, and two plates are included. Also packaged with the machine are four abrasive disks (80-, 150-, 320-, and 1200-grit). The sharpener is belt-driven with ball bearings and a ¼-hp motor; it is stable and quiet. It even comes with its own dust cover. Not much more expensive than a decent grinder, it has the look and feel of quality.

Figure 10-12. Lee Valley's Veritas Mark II system takes adhesive-backed disks from 80- to 1200-grit, and two plates are included.

Dressing grinder wheels

Whenever new wheels are installed, they need to be dressed to remove worn and glazed areas from the face of the stone and reveal new abrasive facets. It also straightens out the edge of the stone, leaving a flat area for sharpening, and a perfectly round and balanced wheel. Most manufacturers recommend a means of dressing their stones, and many include a suitable device with their machines. For the rest, and for most standard bench grinders, there are aftermarket solutions.

One of the most effective dressers is the Wolverine diamond dresser from Oneway Manufacturing (see **Figure 10-13**). It consists of a support arm and a sturdy holder, in which a commercial diamond is placed. The arm slides into the Wolverine jig's base, and the holder is mounted in the support arm. A fine-adjustment knob positions the diamond in relation to the wheel. Dressing the wheel in the required 0.001" increments is easily accomplished by turning the knob one-quarter turn at a time. Oneway's dressing system is the only dresser on the market that allows controlled removal of such a minute amount of material, adding years to the life of a grinding wheel. That opens the door to the option of investing in better, more expensive wheels.

Another viable alternative for dressing is the WheelEzze from Milescraft (see **Figure 10-14**), which is available from woodworking catalog merchants. According to the manufacturer, the "ergonomically designed wheel dressing stick provides a safe and easy solution to dressing any grinding wheel." The large handle allows your entire hand to hold the stick while rotating the cutting medium across the face of a wheel. The silicon carbide medium cleans and contours a wheel, and it has a built-in knuckle guard to keep hands away.

Every now and then, a wheel should be balanced. If there's a lot of wear, or if new wheels are being installed, or if tools bounce a little when they are gently laid on the wheel as it turns, it's time to do this. Once more coming to the rescue, Oneway Manufacturing has developed a balancing system (see **Figure 10-15**) that will compensate for any deviations that would cause wobbling or erratic revolutions. The Oneway kit contains everything needed to balance two wheels.

If there is any flex whatsoever in the tool rests on a grinder, they need to be replaced with sturdy aftermarket versions, such as the Veritas tool rest, shown in **Figure 10-16**. Even one degree of flex will change the angle of a bevel. Worse, it will keep changing every time the operator shifts weight or pressure, so the bevel will end up having more than a single facet.

Figure 10-13. Oneway's wheel dresser has a support arm and a commercial diamond that removes just 0.001" in each pass across the wheel.

Figure 10-14. WheelEzze's silicon carbide medium cleans and contours a wheel, and it even has a built-in knuckle guard.

Figure 10-15. Just like the lead weights hammered onto an auto tire's rim, Oneway's grindstone balancing system stops wobble.

Courtesy Rockler Woodworking & Hardware

Figure 10-16. The Veritas grinder tool rest fits 6" and 8" grinders and many sanders, plus has a 4"-wide rest and an angle-setting jig.

Wet/dry grinding systems

High-speed dry grinding is the fastest way to remove steel, and slow-speed wet grinding is the most controlled way of refining the edge and adding a secondary bevel. Dry grinding and wet grinding machines are available for purchase in addition to combination machines, which have both a dry wheel and a wet wheel. Wet stones, not necessarily whetstones, travel at a small fraction of the speed of dry grinders. The combination of slower speed and constant immersion in cooling water means it's almost impossible to overheat an edge on a modern wet stone. The Tormek system (see **Figure 10-28** on page 84) is a good example of a water-cooled stone, while the Delta is a good example of a machine that has both a high-speed dry wheel and a slow-speed wet one.

Delta

An interesting machine from a very reputable manufacturer, the Delta model 23-710 (see **Figure 10-17**), has both a dry grindstone and a wet honing stone. Its ⅕-hp motor runs a 5"-diameter, 120-grit aluminum oxide dry wheel for grinding, and an eight-inch-diameter, 1,000-grit wet wheel for honing. Both have decent tool rests, and the dry wheel comes with an eye shield. A sliding tool holder that may be used on either wheel secures turning tools, carving chisels, and plane irons. The body is cast iron to reduce vibration, and the wet wheel has front and rear splashguards to control water spray. A companion machine, the Delta 23-725, shown in **Figure 10-7**, is an 8" industrial-grade slow-speed grinder with a ¾-hp motor.

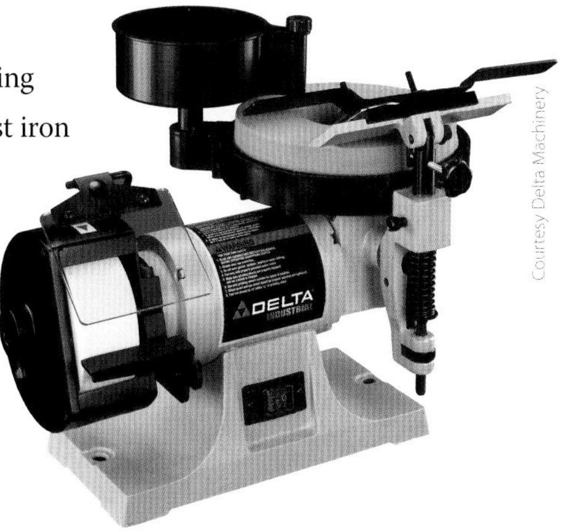

Grizzly Slow-Speed Grinder

Running at an incredibly slow 70 rpm, the larger of the two stones on this Grizzly slow-speed machine (see **Figure 10-18**) is a 10" x 2" white aluminum oxide 220-grit stone. It rotates through a water reservoir to keep things cool, unlike the smaller stone. That's a 100-grit, 4½" x ¾" wheel that spins at 3,450 rpm and is intended for general-purpose grinding. The motor in the G1036 is ¼ hp, 110 volt. The tool rest on the large stone has a couple of locking levers that make adjustments easy and fast. The smaller stone has an eye shield and a tool rest.

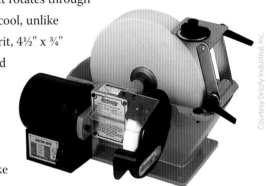

Figure 10-17. The Delta 23-710, an interesting machine from a reputable manufacturer, has both a dry and a wet stone. The machine is 16" wide, 21" deep, and 13" tall, and weighs in at a hefty 42.5 pounds.

Figure 10-18. Grizzly offers a replacement tool rest for wide knives and chisels.

Direction of Rotation

The direction of rotation is an issue in grinding. If the top or side of the grindstone is coming at the operator, grinding is said to be "into the wheel," or "toward the edge." It is a more aggressive, quicker way to grind. If the point of contact on the grindstone is leaving the operator, the tool is said to be ground "out of the wheel," or "away from the edge." This is a safer way to grind because the tool can't dig into the stone and cause damage that could send pieces of stone and tool flying across the shop. However, it can be less controlled, and if the wheel isn't perfectly level, the tool can actually bounce and skip. At the low speed associated with wet grinders, the safety quotient is far less critical than it is with high-speed dry grinding. A wet stone traveling at 100 rpm is a significantly smaller threat than a dry one traveling at 3,450 rpm, so the rotational direction is not as large an issue with wet grinders. Your experience and your comfort level will determine whether rotational direction is an issue for you when shopping for a grinding system.

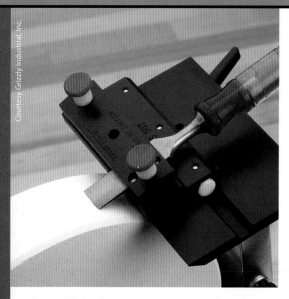

Figure 10-19. Simple and quite compact, the H6069 has a 1¹⁄₂"-wide, 120-grit wheel that turns at 170 rpm through a water bath.

A worm-gear drive mechanism operates both stones at the same time. The machine weighs 32 pounds. The company offers an optional tool rest, which is a sliding support mechanism for sharpening knives and chisels that are wider than the larger wheel. Made by Accu-Sharp, the tool rest (part #G4570, shown in **Figure 10-19**) is fully adjustable and has a positive-lock clamping bracket.

Grizzly Wet Sharpener

At first glance, Grizzly's model H6069 green machine looks like a small barbecue grill (see **Figure 10-20**). Very simple and quite compact, the bench-top wet sharpener has a 1¹⁄₂"-wide, 120-grit wheel that runs very slowly (170 rpm) through a cooling water bath. Forward and reverse controls allow the woodworker to sharpen in either direction, and the machine has a fully adjustable tool rest.

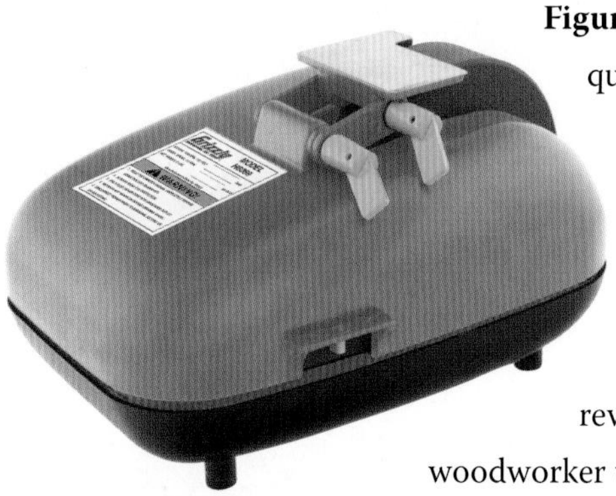

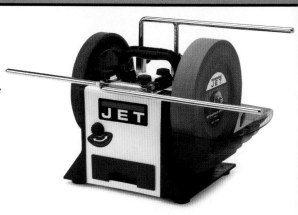

Figure 10-21. JET's 708015 wet grinder features a torque adjustment dial, a variable dial speed, and an oversized water reservoir.

enclosed motor housing keeps debris and water from the interior of the tool, and the basic model comes with a stone grader, a straightedge jig, an angle measurement device, honing compound, a support arm, and a training DVD.

Lap-Sharp

The Lap-Sharp LS-200 (see **Figure 10-22**), a very impressive machine from California-based Wood Artistry LLC. has an American-made, heavy-duty, direct-drive gear motor with needle bearings and a hardened steel shaft. It operates at low speed (under 200 rpm), can be used either wet or dry, and handles abrasive disks down to a very impressive one micron (which is finer than 8,000-grit). The 8"-diameter disks can be changed quickly and are color-coded for easy

Figure 10-22. The standard LS-200 can be used either wet or dry, with 8" abrasive disks down to a very impressive one micron, which corresponds to 8,000-grit.

Figure 10-20. Running at 170 rpm, the large water-cooled stone is 1¹⁄₂" wide and runs through a water bath.

JET

JET's model 708015 slow-speed wet sharpener system (see **Figure 10-21**) features torque adjustment for consistent pressure to the drive shaft, a variable dial speed control that maintains outer wheel speed regardless of the sharpening stone's diameter, and an oversized reservoir for better water management. According to the company, the combination of features is not available on any other system. The machine also is equipped with a tool storage tray and an assortment of eight accessories. Its 1.8 amp

Machines 1: Ergonomics

There are myriad sharpening machines available, but they really boil down to two options: dry bench grinders that grind, and slow wet grinders that hone. Some machines combine the two. For example, the Tormek uses one stone for both grinding and honing, with a special dressing tool that actually changes the grit. Belt sanders can be included in the grinding category (see **Figure 1**) because they work quickly and without water.

Adjusting machines for height is a matter for some thought. It's probably better to err by having the machine too low rather than too high. The most important factor is vision. You must be able to watch the action. For many woodworkers, that can mean being closer to or farther from the work, depending on the state of their eyes (see **Figure 2**). Flood the area with light, and things become more focused. With aging eyes, a wallet-sized magnifier attached to the spark guard is a great help (see **Figure 3**).

Eye protection is imperative. The spark shield must be in place (see **Figure 5**)—it never hurts to clean it—and safety glasses or goggles are essential.

Placing a machine too far back from the edge of a workbench can move the guard out of the line between the stone and your eyes. It also can become uncomfortable because you constantly have to bend to see what's happening.

Since a machine by its very nature does most of the work, the operator's stance and ability to move are lesser concerns than with bench stones. A good stance takes into account the operator's comfort, stability, and the ability to reach the off switch in a hurry in the event anything goes wrong (see **Figure 4**). Neck strings on glasses, drawstrings on sweatshirts, liberated cuffs and shirttails, and loose long hair are all things to avoid around spinning wheels.

Machines should be soundly secured to a stable bench or table. Beyond the obvious safety concerns, a machine that moves will not deliver a uniform grind.

On almost all sharpening machines, the cutter should keep moving back and forth across the wheel so wear on the wheel is as even as possible. There should be enough hand pressure to ensure constant contact all the way across the edge, but not enough to challenge the motor. Some of the slow wet wheels are running with a 1/3-hp motor, and it's easy to stop them with hand pressure (which would, of course, burn out the motor).

When dry grinding, the cutter should be touched to the wheel for no more than a couple of seconds and then quenched in water (see **Figure 6**). Keeping the tool as cool as possible protects the temper and hardness of the steel.

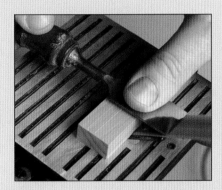

Figure 1. A belt sander can be used in place of a dry grinder.

Figure 2. Position yourself where you can get a clear view of the work, and light it well.

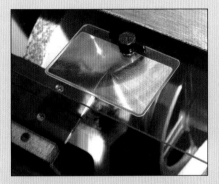

Figure 3. Aging eyes can get a better view with a pocket magnifier attached to the spark guard.

Figure 4. Be certain you can reach the off switch in any emergency.

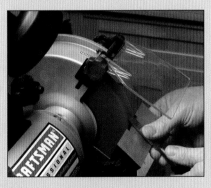

Figure 5. Use the spark shield that came with your grinder, and wear safety glasses or goggles.

Figure 6. On a dry grinder, keep the tool as cool as possible by frequently dipping it in water.

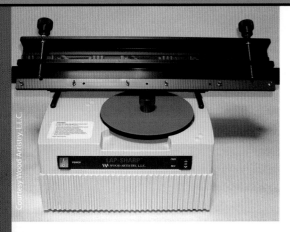

Figure 10-23. The Lap-Sharp has optional accessories that include a tool guide and a planer/jointer knife jig.

Figure 10-24. Makita's model 9820-2 has a 7⁷⁄₈-" stone that spins at 560 rpm, and it will handle knives up to 15³⁄₄" long.

grit identification. The rotation is reversible for sharpening knives, and the machine has optional accessories that include a tool guide, a planer/jointer knife jig (see **Figure 10-23**), a turning and carving gouge jig, a compound honing guide, and even a splash guard. Included with the machine are four color-coded anodized 8" disks, a foot-operated switch, a spray bottle for lubricant, a manual, and an instructional DVD. It has a cast base with a powder-coated finish.

An enhanced version of the LS-200 is available for professional shops. The LS-600VS converts single-phase power to feed a U.S.-made three-phase motor. It has a soft start feature and variable speed that is adjustable from 100 to 600 rpm.

Makita

Although at first glance it looks a lot like the Woodtek machine, the Makita 9820-2 (see **Figure 10-24**) is different in some significant ways. First of all, the wheel is larger (7⁷⁄₈" compared to 8"), and spins a lot faster (560 rpm as opposed to 400 rpm for the Woodtek). Another very quiet machine, it sharpens jointer and planer blades up to 15³⁄₄" long. It comes with an aluminum oxide wheel and draws 1.1 amps. And at 26.9 pounds, it can easily find its way to the job site.

Woodworker David Reed Smith has converted a Makita 9820-2 into a complete sharpening station, shown on page 144. It's well worth a look for anybody who is setting up shop.

Scheppach Grinders

Located in Ichenhausen, Bavaria, the Scheppach Company makes two sharpening machines, the TiGer 2000, shown in **Figure 10-25**, and the TiGer 2500. Similar to the Tormek models, the units form the core of a complete sharpening system using aluminum oxide abrasives. The machines have a solid, powder-coated casing, a splash-proof motor and switches, a removable leather honing wheel, and a nonskid base. The machines come with abrasive paste, an angle guide, and an unbreakable water tank. Scheppach has a considerable presence in the Australian woodworking market.

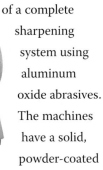

Figure 10-25. There are two models of this superior German machine, the 2000 (household) and the 2500 (professional).

Sharpenset

The Sharpenset is a water-cooled horizontal-wheel system from England (see **Figure 10-26**), and it looks very interesting. A most appropriately named entrepreneur, Arthur Sharp, founded Sharpenset Engineering Ltd. in 1956. The company offers a full line of honing and stropping machines, so they have quite a bit of expertise in this area. There are two optional drill bit sharpening attachments available for

Figure 10-26. The Sharpenset is a British machine from a company with a full line of industrial honing and stropping machines.

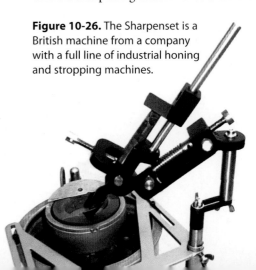

Machines 2: The Sequence

For sharpening hard tool steel, an 8"-inch grinder with a variable or slow speed (1,725 rpm) motor is recommended. The larger wheel leaves less of a hollow grind than a standard 6" wheel, and 3,450 rpm is just too fast for hard steel.

The first step in sharpening on most dry bench grinders is to install the correct wheels (see **Figure 1**). If the grit is too coarse (less than 60-grit), replace the gray stone on the finer wheel with a friable white aluminum oxide stone, preferably 80-grit or 100-grit. The coarse gray wheel supplied with most grinders is far too rough and hard for fine tool steel.

Before you mount the wheel, suspend it on a dowel and tap it with a piece of hardwood. A cracked stone emits a dull thud, while a sound one will ring a clear note. If the stone is cracked, it must be discarded and replaced.

The second step in the sequence is to evaluate the tool rest (see **Figure 2**) and replace it if it is too flimsy. While most factory tool rests have improved quite a bit in recent years, some are still just bent steel that tips to the side a few degrees during use. The tool rest must be completely stable.

Now dress the stone (see **Figure 3**). If the edge isn't square, the cutter won't be. If the stone is clogged or glazed, it won't abrade evenly. If the stone wobbles, replace it or visit the Oneway Website for information on their balancing system. In either case, don't use the grinder. Manually turn the wheel with the machine unplugged, and look for cracks or other damage. A new stone is a lot less expensive than a hospital visit.

It's a good idea to use a permanent marker to mark the area of the cutter that needs to be removed (see **Figure 4**). For that, one needs to have a goal. Is the tool nicked or otherwise damaged and in need of a whole new primary bevel? Or is the cutting edge not at right angles to the sides (see **Figure 5**)? Has the cutter been honed so many times the geometry is off and needs to be re-established? Or do you just want to change from a flat grind to a hollow one? If a chisel or turning tool has been seriously compromised by heat (blue areas extending back from the tip), it may be time to replace

it. Life-saving surgery can be performed by grinding away all of the damaged area and perhaps another one-quarter inch or so of steel (where damage has occurred but isn't visible), but that usually results in further heat buildup and even more damage.

On a dry grinder, less is better. Remove as little material as possible on a dry grinder, while generating as little heat as possible. A visual check is the best way to know when you're done. Measure the bevel angle as you go, using an adjustable square or a protractor (see **Figure 6**), and make minor adjustments if needed. Check for square across the leading edge.

On a slow wet stone, the risk of heat buildup is minimal. To monitor progress, check the angles constantly and feel for a slight burr on the back of the bevel. When the burr extends all the way across, it's time to move along. Many of these machines come with a 1000-grit stone and the manufacturer offers an optional 400-grit one. Changing stones is usually a quick and simple task. Beginning with the coarser stone (400) and finishing with the fine one will deliver a satisfactory edge in a lot less time.

Figure 1. The 8" white aluminum oxide wheel is a full inch wide and is ideal for dry grinding.

Figure 2. Evaluate the tool rest, and if it is flimsy, replace it.

Figure 3. Dress the stone to square its edge and clean its surface.

Figure 4. Mark the metal you intend to grind away.

Figure 5. Be sure the cutting edge is square to the long edge of the blade.

Figure 6. A protractor confirms the grinding angle.

large and small twist bits and an optional parallel attachment, which handles four differently-sized blades up to 20" long, and perhaps longer. A 220-volt to 110-volt adapter is a requirement, and the cost of the system is commensurate with a well-equipped Tormek.

Sherwood Wet/Dry Grinder

The Sherwood wet/dry horizontal grinder (SWG-200) (see **Figure 10-27**) was designed for hand tool sharpening and incorporates two wheels. The first is a dry vertical aluminum oxide grinding wheel that is 50 mm (just under two inches) wide. It runs at 2,850 rpm. The other wheel, a horizontal aluminum oxide stone that is 8" in diameter, runs at 320 rpm for honing.

Figure 10-27.
This Sherwood bench grinder from Timbecon has a dry wheel and a slow wet wheel.

Courtesy Grizzly Industrial, Inc.

Tormek System

Torgny Jansson, a Swedish design engineer, has spent the past thirty-some years creating, developing, and growing the Tormek system (see Figure 10-28). With a unique approach that actively encourages customer feedback, he has spent a great deal of time studying and implementing suggestions from people who use his machines. Jansson has combined the valuable knowledge base with his own research, to the point where his system is perhaps the most comprehensive woodshop sharpening system ever devised. The company has created an astounding range of jigs and optional devices that address virtually every specialty need: jigs for planer and jointer knives, molding heads, gouges, axes, scissors, long and short tools, and so on. The system includes the necessary equipment for dressing the wheel (with a diamond dresser), renewing a glazed stone, leather honing, and it includes educational materials.

While the key to the system is the SuperGrind 2000, a smaller version, the SuperGrind 1200, shown in **Figure 10-29**, is designed for grinding

Figure 10-28. The Tormek SuperGrind 2000 has a welded steel housing, a 10" x 2" stone, and a 90-rpm motor, and weighs about 31 pounds.

Figure 10-29. The Tormek SuperGrind 1200 has a plastic housing, an 8" x ⁵⁄₈" stone, and a 120-rpm motor, and weighs 15.4 pounds.

and sharpening hand tools, including carving tools, and it accepts all the jigs.

Equipped with an aluminum oxide grindstone and a leather honing wheel, the SuperGrind 2000's axle rotates at just 90 rpm. In addition to negating the buildup of excessive heat, the slow speed offers a great deal of control. There is time to react. And at this speed, changes are visible and can be addressed before they become problems.

Machines 3: Grinding

Woodworkers tend to inherit tools, or buy them used, or permanently borrow them from people who just don't deserve them. Many tools need some work, and the first step is often to remove rust and grime with a motorized wire wheel (see **Figure 1**). When doing this, one should wear safety glasses or goggles because wire wheels (like some woodworkers) have a habit of losing their hair.

The second step is to flatten the back of each cutter or tool within an inch or so of the cutting edge. If the edge is nicked, grind it square in a series of very short contacts with the wheel (see **Figure 2**). Heat is the enemy. Work for a few seconds, and then paddle the blade in cooling water. Remember, by the time a blade turns blue, heat has drawn out the temper from the steel, making it too brittle to hold an edge.

Both ends of a grinder's arbor spin in the same direction. The top of the wheel is coming at the operator as the bottom moves away. Grinding is done at the top of the wheel where a tool rest, the angle of address, and the hardness of the stone all prevent the blade from digging in. With a soft leather or cotton wheel, a sharp tool would immediately dig into the fabric, causing it to be torn from the operator's hands. For this reason, buffing and stropping take place below the arbor, as the wheel is leaving (see **Figure 3**). The same is true of wire wheels.

Vertical grindstones must contact the tool on their edge, and never on their sides. Slow wet wheels are designed for contact on their sides because they rest on a support system. A vertical stone travels too fast and is unsupported. Using the side of a dry stone is a recipe for injury. It weakens the stone and can cause it to shatter. At 1,725 rpm, the edge of an 8" stone is traveling a mile every 88 seconds.

A grinder should never be run without the guards in place. In addition, the tool rest should be no more than ⅛" away from the stone, and preferably less (see **Figure 4**). The spark deflector should also always be in place. Don't ever touch a revolving stone with your fingers, even a slow wet one, because it will immediately begin to abrade skin. And never stand directly in front of a grinder when it is starting up because if a stone is flawed and about to shatter, start-up is when it is liable to do so.

A blade with a sharp edge that is not square (at 90 degrees) to its sides will tend to wander as it works through wood (see **Figure 5**). When a woodworker hits such a chisel with a mallet, the point will bite first, and then the rest of the blade will slide toward the point, diminishing control. It also will deliver a cut that is out of square. A plane iron out of square can gouge a surface or leave a score mark (see **Figure 6**). Unevenly ground tools that are turning have a mind of their own. An off-center gouge will take a walk along the turning, or it may chatter. It may scrape powder along one side of the bevel and peel shavings with the other.

Figure 1. With a much-abused tool, the first step is to remove rust and grime using a wire wheel.

Figure 2. Square up the edge and remove nicks on a coarse wheel, frequently cooling the tool in water.

Figure 3. Wire brushing, buffing, and stropping take place on the part of the wheel that travels away from the tool, not toward it.

Figure 4. The tool rest should be very close to the wheel.

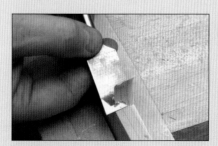

Figure 5. An edge that is not square to its sides will wander out of control.

Figure 6. An out-of-square plane iron will be difficult to adjust and may carve a track in the work.

The Tormek machine uses a universal tool rest that can be mounted on the top or the front of the machine, as shown in **Figure 10-32**. It is essentially a steel bar to which all of the various jigs and fixtures are attached. These hold the tool or cutter at a specific angle from which it cannot deviate. This enables forming a uniform edge because the jig both establishes and then maintains the required angle.

There is some adjustment in almost every Tormek jig, and the tool rest is micro-adjustable. The adjustment is necessary because not all blades have the same dimensions. This is perhaps the only aspect of the Tormek system that is not completely intuitive—it requires a little experience and judgment. However, the company provides a comprehensive, well-written, 150-page manual with hundreds of crystal clear

Figure 10-31. Most jigs for a Tormek attach to the universal support, a bar that can be placed on top or in front of the unit.

instructions and also offers support through their Website. Tormek's literature uses perfectly acceptable definitions of grinding and honing that may be confusing to American ears: Grinding seems to include everything up to final stropping on a leather wheel, which they term "honing."

Woodtek

The Woodtek water-cooled sharpening machine (see **Figure 10-32**) was designated a "top value" by *Wood* magazine in 2002. The compact unit takes up less than one square foot of bench space. The 7"-diameter, 1,000-grit wheel spins at 420 rpm for very smooth, precise sharpening. An adjustable built-in guide makes it easy to set the correct angle for any type of edge. It weighs 13 pounds and will accommodate a range of stone grits. The Woodtek sharpener is quite inexpensive. I purchased one a couple of years ago and ordered a second, 400-grit wheel for more aggressive grinding, with impressive results. As

M.Power Sharpener

Not strictly a "machine" because it isn't motorized, the M.POWER Precision Sharpening System (PSS1), shown in **Figure 10-30**, is a tough, aluminum device that includes two DMT monocrystalline diamond abrasive stones. The base of the unit holds a blade or chisel stationary while the top, set at a fixed angle (25 or 30 degrees), guides the diamond abrasive across the tool's bevel. Included are a prep stone and a finishing stone. The geometry of the gadget means that the sharpening action takes place parallel to the cutting edge, which is 90 degrees different from other sharpening machines. This is just about the simplest sharpening device on the market, and certainly one of the most effective. It is almost as fast as a bench grinder for creating or maintaining a primary bevel, prior to establishing a secondary one with a fine polishing water stone.

Figure 10-30. The DMT M.POWER PSS1 is a tough, aluminum device with two monocrystalline diamond abrasive stones.

Figure 10-32. The Woodtek water-cooled sharpener spins at 420 rpm and comes with a 1,000-grit wheel.

with all slow grinders, it takes a while to learn enough patience to allow the stone to do its job. You tend to push the tool into its path in an effort to sense the familiar sound and feel of a regular bench grinder. That can lead you to believe the machines are underpowered, which simply isn't true. They are doing the job without generating excess heat. The Woodtek machine comes with a ⅙-hp (1.2-amp) motor, which is plenty of power for the job it is being asked to do.

Power sanders

Belt sanders can be very useful for rough grinding and rapid removal of metal, and as you will see with the JoolTool in **Figure 10-34**, what is basically a sanding machine can be capable of very fine work as well.

Disk sanders, whether stand-alone or integrated units such as the Shopsmith, can do a fair job grinding, but they generate heat rather quickly. Results depend on the speed the disk is traveling, the type and grit of the abrasive, and the condition of the machine. Having owned a Shopsmith for almost 20 years, my personal opinion is bench stones work best for fine honing. Other Shopsmith owners may disagree. It is, however, a remarkable machine for almost all of its other functions. The drill press, in particular, is beautifully engineered and is a dream to strop with because of its variable speed, lack of run-out, and large, adjustable table.

Delta

Raymond Lanham, a remarkable turner from Texas, has attached a one-inch Delta belt sander to his lathe, as shown in **Figure 10-33**. He runs zirconia belts on it, which he purchases from Lee Valley Tools. These blue zirconia sharpening belts are a combination of aluminum oxide and zirconium oxide. The abrasive is extremely hard, long lasting, and very resistant to particle dulling. The belts are designed to grind hardened steel of all kinds, including stainless, and they can put a

Figure 10-33.
Small belt sanders, with the right zirconia/aluminum oxide belts, can be very useful in grinding and even honing.

Courtesy Raymond Latham

very nice edge on high-speed steel turning tools. They are available in 40-grit, 80-grit, and 120-grit, and in 30" and 42" lengths. The length of the belt helps somewhat in keeping the tool cool, and the table on the small sanders tilts at an angle for various bevels. Lee Valley also offers 15-micron silicon carbide belts, which will leave a near mirror finish.

Not all woodworkers trust the platen on small belt sanders. This is a little piece of metal behind the belt, and the problem is there is flex in the lighter versions. Before investing, it is worth checking. It may have to be reinforced.

JoolTool

The JoolTool is a strange-looking device (see **Figure 10-34**) that, on first glance, would probably appear more at home in a kitchen than a workshop. Don't let that innocent culinary disguise look fool you. The little machine is a compact, multi-functional tool perfect for grinding, sharpening, sanding, deburring, polishing, and much more. Originally designed with jewelers in mind, it

Figure 10-34. The JoolTool allows the woodworker to look down through the strange disks and actually see an edge being ground.

Courtesy Jooltool.com

has become very popular among woodworkers who attend trade shows and have seen it in person. The company has worked directly with 3M to develop its system, a dry, cool, compound-free way to sharpen. They even have polishing brushes.

The magic of the JoolTool is that one can look down through the top and actually watch the edge being ground or polished. A woodworker holds a tool up against those strange-looking disks, and he or she can actually see through the gaps between the fingers. Included with the machine are a tapered spindle and abrasive disks in several grits, plus buffing and polishing wheels and brushes. The Website is *jooltool.com*.

Figure 10-35. Oscillating sanders, such as the Ridgid model shown here, wear well, run cool, and offer good dust collection

Figure 10-36. On the Ridgid sander, the front table drops to 45 degrees, creating some possibilities for gouge and scraper sharpening.

Ridgid

Another option for coarse grinding is a larger, oscillating belt sander like the one shown in **Figure 10-35**. The machine has a short belt, but because it oscillates up and down, the belt stays cool. The front table on the Ridgid model swings down 45 degrees (see **Figure 10-36**), which isn't enough for most sanding. However, it may be enough to mount a shop-built jig that would bring the bevel angle to 25 degrees. One small disadvantage is the platen behind the belt stops shy of the pulley at the end of the belt. There is a small gap in the support where the two almost meet, so feeding tools from the end of the belt is a bit uncontrolled. Even a slight wobble can throw off the angle of a secondary bevel.

Drill bit sharpeners

Drill bits are particularly tedious to sharpen by hand because it is all too easy to destroy their cutting angles and grind them off center. That explains the popularity of dedicated little machines for drill bit sharpening, such as the ones shown here.

Drill Doctor

The Drill Doctor XP, shown in **Figure 10-37**, is an upgrade on a traditional favorite among woodworkers. The efficient new unit sharpens ³⁄₃₂" to ½" twist bits in about a minute, or even less. It handles high-speed steel, masonry, carbide, cobalt, TiN-coated, and masonry bits. The machine also will create a split-point bit for faster penetration and less drill bit wandering.

Figure 10-37. The Drill Doctor XP sharpens ³⁄₃₂" to ½" twist bits in about a minute and works on HSS, carbide, and more.

Figure 10-38. The HDC sharpener is a very inexpensive double-insulated machine from Homier that runs a $^1/_{10}$-hp motor.

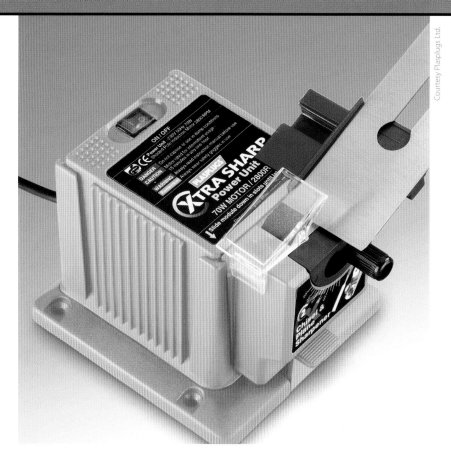

HDC Drill Bit Sharpener

The HDC 02777 drill bit sharpener (see **Figure 10-38**) is an inexpensive double-insulated machine from Homier that runs a $^1/_{10}$-hp motor at 1,600 rpm and weighs about 5 pounds. Its 80-grit abrasive sharpens carbon steel and high-speed steel bits from $^9/_{64}$" to $^{25}/_{64}$".

Plasplugs System

The Plasplugs system, from Britain, is quite inexpensive and is being marketed in the United States with the endorsement of Dean Johnson, star of PBS television's *Hometime* show. The concept is that a small motor and an aluminum oxide grinding wheel are housed in the main unit, and various modules can be attached to the front to handle sharpening tasks including drill bits (see **Figure 10-39**) and knives, as well as planes and chisels (see **Figure 10-40**). The drill bit unit resharpens 25 sizes of standard high-speed steel drill bits, from $^7/_{64}$" to $^3/_8$". Each module acts as a custom jig to hold the tool at the correct angle for sharpening.

Figure 10-40. Another module for the Plasplugs machine, the plane- and chisel-sharpening unit slides tools across the wheel.

Figure 10-39. An inexpensive British import, the Plasplugs machine has several modules including this one for twist drill bits.

CHAPTER 11

Sharpening Methods

The various options for sharpening include oil, water, and ceramic bench stones, and a variety of machines and jigs, as discussed in previous chapters. If you already own some equipment, read through the relevant chapters to learn about the characteristics, properties, and agents (oil or water) that apply to your specific stones and setup. If you're ready to invest in some equipment, those chapters will help guide your decisions.

My personal preference is to use a motorized horizontal water stone and a slow 8" bench grinder with a medium to fine friable wheel for grinding (creating the shape of the tool), diamond bench stones and slips for the early stages of sharpening, fine water stones for honing, and a charged cotton wheel for buffing. My sharpening setup is shown in **Figure 11-1**.

Figure 11-1. The author's sharpening setup features a horizontal water stone, a slow 8" bench grinder with a medium to fine friable wheel, diamond bench stones and slips, fine water stones for honing, and a charged cotton wheel for buffing.

Five kinds of tools

From a sharpening point of view, woodworking tools can be divided into five broad categories:

- bench tools,
- turning tools,
- carving tools,
- mattocks, and
- machine cutters.

This chapter walks you step-by-step through a typical sharpening session for each category, addressing as many shapes and angles as you're likely to meet. Before we get to specifics, there are a few things to keep in mind.

Grinding isn't always necessary. If a tool just needs a quick touchup, skip past the grinding steps in each of the following sections, and go straight to honing. Grinding establishes the angle, while honing maintains it. Turning is different from carving and general woodworking. Turners generally grind and buff (see **Figure 11-2**), but they skip the honing stage on many of their tools (more on this later).

It's important to know when to move from one grit to the next. There are few shop experiences as rewarding as being able to shave the back of your hand after the final stropping of an edge (see **Figure 11-3**). When it cuts hair, it's ready to cut wood.

While that has long been the woodworker's traditional test of an edge, there are a couple of safer ways to know when it's time to move along. With your fingertips, touch the back of the edge and you'll feel a small steel burr being formed. When it extends uniformly all the way across the edge, you have removed enough steel.

When you're getting close to being finished with honing, look directly at the edge with a light behind you and a little to one side. If you can't see it, no matter how you tilt and squint, it's sharp. A perfect edge reflects no light. If you can see a shine or reflection, you're not quite done. A flat edge reflects light off its dull spots. A sharp edge hasn't any dull spots.

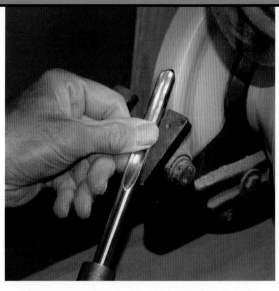

Figure 11-2. Master turners such as Ellis Hein, shown here shaping a gouge, often use only a grinder and strop to sharpen.

Figure 11-3. Traditionally, the ultimate test of a freshly honed edge has been to shave the hairs on the back of one's hand.

Another way to judge whether the edge is good enough is to do what Norm Abram does: Slice through a sheet of paper you're holding in the air in one hand, while holding the tool in the other. If the edge shears the paper without resistance, it's time to work wood.

Patient sharpening is part of the whole woodshop experience. Learning to enjoy it is magic—being able to transform a chore into a treat. After all, how many other hobbies have the word "working" in their name?

Sharpening Sessions: Bench Tools

Cabinet Scrapers, Bench Chisels, Planes, Spokeshaves

Common bench tools can be grouped into four types:

- cabinet scrapers,
- bench chisels,
- planes, and
- spokeshaves.

Bench tools are the mainstay of furniture making. They are used to flatten, smooth, and shape wooden parts, and to cut joints in them. Cabinet scrapers are different from the other three types of bench tool in that their edges are ground straight across, and then burnishing the steel raises a cutting burr. The others all have blades that are flat on the back and beveled on the front, with a sharp secondary bevel honed at the very tip.

Cabinet scrapers (card scrapers)

Among the simplest of woodworking tools, cabinet scrapers are nothing more than flat pieces of steel. They come in various shapes, and while the most popular is a simple rectangle, other profiles can match moldings and edge treatments (see **Figure 11-4**). They are a gift from the gods when it comes to taming wild grain because they scrape a very thin layer off the top of the wood. Crown Tools made the scrapers in England, from the finest Sheffield steel. They are stored with a very light coat of oil. To use a scraper, hold it in two hands, perpendicular to the surface of the wood. Press with your thumbs to flex the scraper into the smallest of arcs. Scrapers are sometimes pulled, but most often are pushed, across the wood. A scraper plane has a cast-iron or wooden holder that looks like a block plane or a spokeshave with the blade flexed and locked in place. Some of the tools have a beveled edge on the blade, but it's sharpened in the same way as the more common card scraper.

Bench chisels

Flat bench chisels are a joy to sharpen. They can be ground and honed in minutes, and restored from just about any abuse the world can throw at them. The edge of a sharp chisel is formed by the intersection of two flat planes: the flat back of the chisel, and the honed bevel on the front of the chisel. The key to sharpness is to reduce the intersection of these two planes to a point where there is essentially no resistance as they work wood.

Figure 11-4. Cabinet scrapers, such as this Sheffield steel set from Crown Tools, come in a variety of shapes.

New Device for Grinding

The PSS1 diamond sharpener from M.POWER (see **Figure 11-5**) is a nontraditional option for grinding the primary bevel. This aluminum device holds a chisel or a plane iron at either 25 degrees (primary bevel) or 30 degrees (secondary bevel). A tray holds the tool while a sled carries various grits of diamond-coated sharpeners across the bevel. The sharpeners are manufactured by one of the leaders in this field, Diamond Machining Technologies (DMT).

Courtesy M.Power Tools

Figure 11-5. An amazingly simple tool, the M.POWER PSS1 combines diamond abrasives and an aluminum jig with preset angles.

Step 1. Clamp the scraper firmly in a vise and square up all the edges with a coarse stone or a file. Here, I'm using a coarse diamond bench stone. Work across each edge at 90 degrees, back and forth with measured, even strokes.

Step 2. For curved edges, use a diamond cone or a round diamond file. This creates a flat edge, which would actually work for a while. However, the next step in preparing a scraper makes if far more effective in use.

Step 3. A small burr increases the effect, and the useful life, of a scraper's edge. Create it by rolling over the edges, using a piece of steel that is harder than the scraper. This action is known as burnishing. Half a dozen strokes should do the job. During the first stroke, hold the burnisher parallel to the scraper's edge, and on each of the following strokes, raise the handle one or two degrees, working one side and then the other.

Step 4. Test the scraper on some scrap hardwood. The edge should produce shavings, not powder.

Step 1. Use a medium-grit belt sander to remove years of grime and rust along the length of a chisel, and do it in the blink of an eye. The trick is to keep the chisel moving back and forth at a pretty good clip, while lightly touching it against the drum, or against the belt as it passes across the platen.

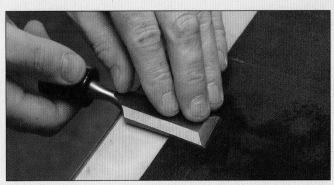

Step 2. With the blade cleaned up, sharpening can begin. Use a lapping plate (see page 48), or a set of flat bench stones to flatten the back (the face without a bevel). Work down through coarse and medium grits, concentrating on the last inch or so closest to the cutting edge. You won't be using fine grits until Step 4.

Courtesy Scheppach GmbH

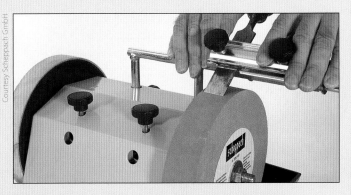

Step 3. Create or repair the primary (main) bevel using an aggressive method such as a very coarse diamond bench stone for a flat grind, or a friable 60-grit wheel on a bench grinder for a hollow grind (see page 74 for a discussion on flat and hollow grinds). A slow wet wheel works well, too. It's not as quick, but there's less chance of overheating the chisel. Generally speaking, grind chisels at 25 degrees (and hone a secondary bevel at about 28 degrees, which we'll get to in a minute).

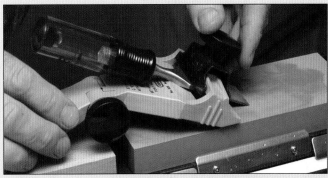

Step 4. The most enjoyable way to hone a secondary bevel is on a series of fine water stones—1,000-, 4,000-, and 8,000-grits will do nicely. A jig is pretty much essential. An alternative is to raise the angle of the tool rest on a wet grinder to 28 degrees, and gently slide the chisel onto the stone. Your bench stones will raise a small burr along the back of the edge. You can feel it with your fingertip and see it under magnification. It must extend all the way across the edge.

Step 5. Once a burr has been raised, lay the flat back of the chisel on a polishing stone (8000-grit or your finest available) and gently remove the burr. Then return to the bevel side of the chisel and continue working it through the grits until you reach the finest stone.

Step 6. Complete the secondary bevel by stropping on a charged leather wheel, making sure the bevel (and not the tip) is being stropped. Leather strops have a habit of creeping over the edge the first few times somebody uses them. A buffing wheel will polish the steel and remove scratches, but a charged leather strop will actually refine the edge.

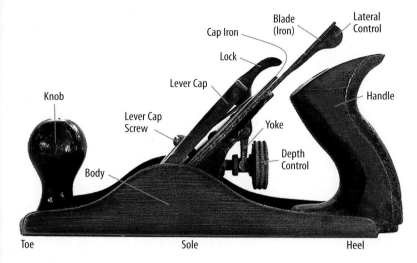

Figure 11-6. Most bench planes follow the architecture shown here, changing little more than the pitch and the length of the sole.

Planes

The first time somebody uses a plane, the odds are pretty slim he or she will have a poetic experience, where the shavings magically ribbon out of the tool. However, the more one works at it, the more it works. After a while, electric sanders begin to gather dust as one reaches more and more for a hand plane to tame wild boards. This is the very essence of woodworking (see **Figure 11-6**).

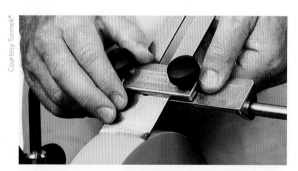

Figure 11-7. At 2" wide, the slow wet wheel on a Tormek SuperGrind 2000 is an excellent choice for sharpening plane irons.

Courtesy Tormek®

Figure 11-8. With five abrasive grits available on quick-change plates, the M.POWER PSS1 will handle plane irons up to 2½" wide.

Courtesy M.Power Tools

Plane irons can be sharpened on slow grinders with jigs designed for this purpose (see **Figure 11-7**), and this is an excellent way to create or maintain a primary bevel. So, too, is the M.POWER sharpener (see **Figure 11-8**), which will deliver a very nice primary bevel of 25 degrees across the edge. But for truly great results, and a most enjoyable experience, a plane needs to be tuned. That means lapping the sole (abrading the bottom) of it until it is perfectly flat, and then sharpening and setting the blade.

Spokeshaves

Spokeshaves are flat, concave, or convex, as shown in **Figure 11-9**. A double shave combines two of the shapes. Sharpen the flat blades much like plane irons; sharpening the curved blades requires some shop-made aids. Even with aids, convex and concave shapes are sharpened freehand, without the angle being locked in by a jig, so they require practice.

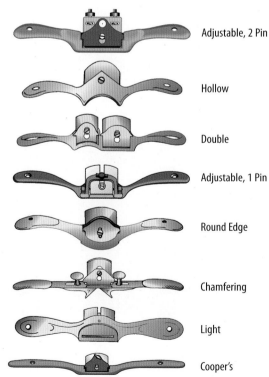

Figure 11-9. Spokeshaves are manufactured in a wide variety of styles for making shapes and curves.

▲ **Step 1**. Lap the plane sole on lapping plates. These are pieces of ¼" plate glass with wet/dry sandpaper attached to them with two-sided tape or spray adhesive. For a detailed discussion of lapping and sandpaper, see page 48. Color the sole (bottom of the plane) with a felt marker, dribble a few drops of water on the lapping plates, and work down through the grits until the marker color disappears completely. Don't remove the blade and cap iron. Retard the blade so it doesn't protrude, but leave it in the plane to maintain normal tension, or the sole won't ever be flat.

▲ **Step 2**. Flatten the back (the face with no bevel) on the lapping plates. You need to flatten only the ½" to 1" nearest to the cutting edge. After lapping, work down through the grits from your coarsest stone to your finest.

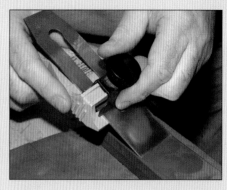

▲ **Step 3**. To grind the primary bevel, set a honing guide to 25 degrees and work down through the stones from coarse to medium. Move the iron around on the stone to avoid wearing grooves (see page 24).

▲ **Step 4**. Reset the guide for two more degrees to 27 degrees for softwoods, while 28 degrees is better for harder species. Repeat the honing process to create a secondary bevel. It should be about 1/8" wide. Work all the way down to a polishing water stone of at least 4000 grit, and preferably 8000 (in oilstones, a hard black Arkansas is a close equivalent).

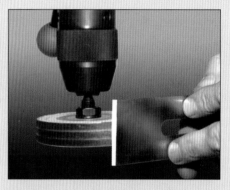

▲ **Step 5**. Charge a stropping wheel with Flexcut Gold or a similar compound, and pass the blade quickly across it, removing the tiny burr left by very fine stones. The wheel should be running slowly, 200 to 300 rpm. You can replace this step by using a cotton buffing wheel on a bench grinder, using the same compound.

▲ **Step 6**. The cap iron and the lever cap of a plane secure the iron. Run a diamond hone across the lever cap to make sure it's perfectly flat before you place the cap iron below it. Also flatten the cap iron where it contacts the blade, using a flat stone or the lapping plate. The cap iron has to have full contact all the way across the blade, must be positioned so that it guides and breaks up shavings as they form, and must prevent shavings from being trapped between itself and the blade. Any gap whatsoever between the blade and the cap iron will jam the plane with shavings and slivers on the second or third stroke.

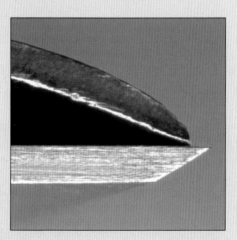

◀ **Step 7**. Assemble the plane with as little as possible of the iron (blade) protruding below the sole. Place the cap iron correctly before locking it in place: A good starting spot is 1/16" up from the cutting edge of the blade, and experiment from there for perfect results. The first mistake that new woodworkers make with planes is having the iron protrude too far, forcing the plane to take a thick slice of wood instead of a shaving. By starting with almost no contact and slowly increasing the exposure, you can reach a spot where the plane takes thin, uniform ribbons with virtually no resistance.

Step 1. Flatten the back of the blade using a sequence of coarse, medium, and fine bench stones. Only the half of the blade closest to the cutting edge needs to be worked. A blade won't require flattening again unless it has been subjected to undue heat, or has been somehow nicked or damaged.

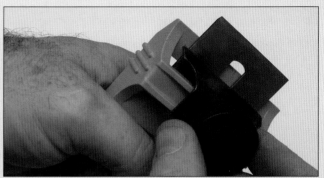

Step 2. Lock the blade into a jig (the trusty old General 908 is shown) and set the angle. Some more sophisticated jigs have special holders for short blades. The best angle is about 30 degrees, although anything from 25 degrees (softwood) to 35 degrees (dense hardwoods) will work.

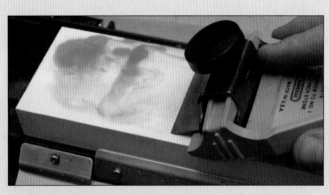

Step 3. Work down through the grits from your coarsest bench stone to your finest, keeping in mind that only one bevel is required here. Vary the pattern and keep the stone well charged with oil or water, depending on its cleaning agent. Change grits when a burr forms across the entire edge. Remove the burr by rubbing the back of the blade across the next finer stone. Remove the final burr with a strop or buffing wheel.

Step 4. Sharpen concave (hollow) blades by finding a cylinder with the same radius as the curve on the blade. Apply wet/dry sandpaper to the cylinder to create a form. Large dowels may work, or a form can be quickly turned to the correct diameter on a lathe. Secure the blade in a vise and work the edge through several grits, beginning with 220 and working toward 1,000 or even finer, if you can find it. Keep the paper wet to avoid filling the small pores in the closed grit.

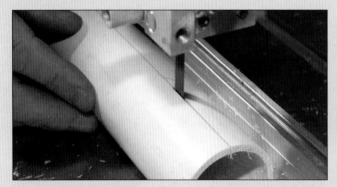

Step 5. Sharpen convex (round) blades just like the concave ones, except that you need an inside curve for the form. Plastic plumbing pipe will often work because it comes in many sizes. Slice the pipe along its length to make the form.

Step 6. Assemble the spokeshave and test it on softwood. If the shaving is transparent and crumbles, you can probably let out more of the blade. If the tool stutters and digs in, retract the blade a little. In clear wood, perfect shavings are continuous, are uniform in thickness across the blade, and curl tightly.

Sharpening Sessions: Turning Tools

Gouges, Skews, Scrapers, Parting Tools

As you can see in **Figure 11-10**, turning tools are manufactured in enormous variety. For our purposes, however, they can be categorized in five groups:

- roughing gouges,
- spindle, bowl, and detail gouges,
- skews,
- scrapers, and
- specialty items, such as parting tools.

Figure 11-10. Turning tools include skews, parting tools, bowl and spindle gouges, and scrapers. Each requires its own sharpening regimen.

The tools all are used in various styles of spindle and faceplate turning to establish the initial cylindrical surface, then to shape and detail it for finishing. Each type of tool requires a specific sharpening regimen. The sharpening of most turning tools is primarily a grinding operation since contact with the spinning workpiece almost instantly blunts a finely honed edge.

In addition to the standard tools discussed here, there are a number of very specialized turning tools available, such as thin box scrapers, chatter tools, spiraling and texture tools. All of the tools have specific sharpening regimens and rigid geometries. Before sharpening or reshaping any of these tools, check the manufacturer's instructions.

Since a gouge is usually the first tool that a turner reaches for, let's begin there.

Roughing gouges

Roughing gouges are primarily used between centers to turn a blank into a cylinder, and the grind on them is simple. A brand-new roughing gouge is usually ground at 90 degrees across at the factory, with a 45-degree bevel shaped along the outside edge. As with most turning tools, gouge sharpening is primarily a grinding operation that is most easily done on a spinning wheel rather than on bench stones. Some advanced sharpening systems have jigs to help maintain the shape of the tool and its bevel angle, as shown in **Figure 11-11** and **Figure 11-12**.

Courtesy Scheppach GmbH

Figure 11-11. The slow-speed, water-cooled Scheppach grinder comes with a jig for maintaining the bevel angle on a roughing gouge.

Courtesy Wood Artistry, L.L.C.

Figure 11-12. For turners, the Lap-Sharp offers a huge array of abrasive disks and delivers a flat grind rather than a hollow grind.

Step 1. Set the tool rest on the grinder to 90 degrees, and square off the end in short contacts with the stone. Repeatedly quench the tool in cool water to avoid any heat buildup.

Step 2. Set the tool rest to 45 degrees and grind a new bevel on the end. Roll the gouge back and forth, spending a hair more time on the outside edges than on the center. The rolling motion means the center of the edge is likely to spend more time in contact with the wheel than the ends, so to avoid overgrinding, speed up a little there. If have two grits of stone on your grinder, do most of the grinding on the finer one. Check the edge by looking straight at it: You are looking for an edge that doesn't reflect light (no flat spots).

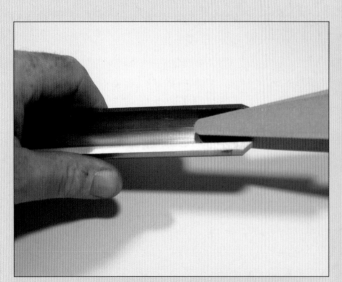

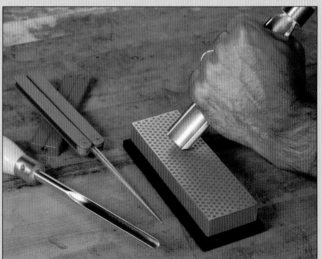

Step 3. Use a shaped slip stone or 400-grit wet/dry sandpaper wrapped on a dowel (choose one that is as close to the inside diameter of the gouge as possible) to remove the burr created by grinding. Water isn't necessary, but if you do use any, make sure the gouge is completely dry before you store it.

Step 4. Keep a coarse bench stone handy for touchups between grinding. In use, a roughing gouge usually wears down quickest in the center, while the sides hold an edge longer. A quick dressing of the center every now and then means that you won't have to stop and grind so often.

Courtesy DMT®, Diamond Machining Technology

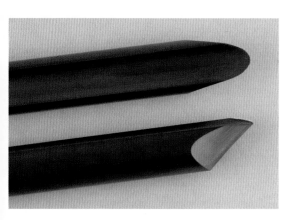

Spindle, bowl, and detail gouges

Spindle and bowl gouges are somewhat interchangeable. You can use a bowl gouge to turn a spindle, but the reverse isn't always true, or comfortable. They look similar, but as shown in **Figure 11-13**, the sides of a spindle gouge are not as tall as the sides of a bowl gouge. The bowl gouge has the deepest flute, and the detail tool is essentially a small version of the bowl gouge, with a spindle gouge's grind.

The precise angles for grinding the three gouges are somewhat subjective, but Doug Thompson, the maker of the tools shown in Figure 11-13, does it as shown. You would not be far wrong to follow these angles with gouges from other manufacturers.

Thompson's gouges have more steel under the flute than those of other manufacturers, creating a strong tool that's easy to control, especially when extended far over the tool rest. In general, bowl gouges are made with greater tensile and shear strength than spindle gouges because they are designed to reach further past the support of the tool rest without vibrating or snapping. Snapping is a remote possibility at best, but turning without adequate tool rest support is a dangerous practice, and you can buy or make curved rests that reach into the work to support a bowl gouge close to its tip. Lathe tools can, in the 1867 words of George Leybourne, a British lyricist, "fly through the air with the greatest of ease."

"Bowl gouges," Thompson says, "are a balance between flute shape and depth to prevent clogging." In addition to their thickness, Thompson's tools have a gunmetal finish that results from heat treatment. He also uses a high-vanadium steel hardened to 60-62 Rockwell and triple tempered with a cryogenic treatment between the first and second temper to increase durability and toughness.

Given the shape of gouges, there are limitations on the profiles that you could grind. For most purposes, a traditional fingernail grind will meet

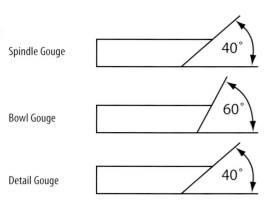

Spindle Gouge — 40°

Bowl Gouge — 60°

Detail Gouge — 40°

Figure 11-13. Three gouges by toolmaker Doug Thompson show the difference between a spindle gouge (top), a bowl gouge (center), and a detail gouge (bottom). Photo courtesy Thompson Lathe Tools.

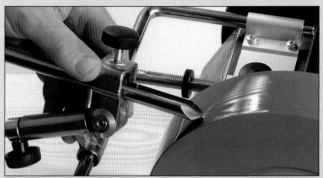

Step 1. Familiarize yourself with the fingernail profile. It has been around a very long time, but as each new generation of turners discovers it, they add to the lore.

Step 2. Choose a jig. The sides of the fingernail shape will need more grinding than the tip. The action, therefore, is more elliptical than circular. Various jigs will give you control of this, among them the Wolverine, Ellsworth, Sorby, and Tru-Grind, all of which are discussed and shown in Chapter 9: Angles and Jigs, and the Tormek, shown here.

Step 3. Set the angle. Like this Sorby jig, all gouge jigs trap the tool in a mobile holder that moves the tip in an elliptical pattern (rather than a simple circle) against the stone, so you can choose how much side grind to add. Be aware that the diameter of your stone might affect the geometry. A friable white wheel doesn't create as much heat as a gray one, and it sharpens faster.

Step 4. Present the inside curve of the newly formed edge to a charged buffing or stropping wheel for a few seconds to chase the burr and polish the grind. Doing so will give you better shearing action for a little while, and you can repeat the process several times between grinds.

Step 1. Using the tool rest on your grinder, shape the leading edge of the gouge with a gentle curve, which looks like the profile of a fingernail from the side. It slopes in the neighborhood of 25 degrees (bowls) to 30 degrees (spindles), but these are only starting suggestions. Some jig manufacturers call out these angles in terms of the slope on the tool (65 degrees and 60 degrees, respectively), rather than the tool rest angle. Depending on the species and grain you turn, the profiles that you cut, and the size of the work, your experience will lead you to vary these angles, perhaps substantially.

Step 2. To add a gentle sweep along the sides, you may need to set an extreme angle on the tool rest so most of it is out of the way. Slide the gouge up the wheel as you grind the sides, and down the wheel as you turn through the tip. Blend the side grinds into the walls of the tool. Turners who work very delicate turnings prefer to grind a sharper point and work the wings a long way back to maximize the cutting area.

your needs. The grind is so named simply because it resembles a fingernail. The version shown in Step 1 below is for spindle gouges. For bowls, the sides can sweep back further to include a side grind for deeper work. The fingernail grind can be done freehand on a tool rest, but I recommend using a jig, which is more controlled and far safer. Freehand grinding is not a great way to start out, because more than one gouge has ended up a lot shorter than the woodturner wanted, and a few have landed in the shop wall.

Turners who have been grinding the fingernail profile for a long time eventually do learn how to do so without a jig, as shown in **Figure 11-14**. The results may not be as uniform as with a jig, but they are more readily customizable. People at this skill level visualize the finished grind, and through long experience know how to tweak it. Master turner Cindy Drozda, for example, grinds some gouges almost to a point because she works on small and delicate turnings with minute detailing (see **Figure 11-15**).

Figure 11-14. Cindy Drozda sharpens a spindle gouge in her studio near Boulder, Colorado.

Fingernail Grind on a Tormek

Torgny Jansson introduced a new little jig in late 2006, the Tormek Setter TTS-100, a plastic layout device designed to help turners with the fingernail grind. It allows for exact replication of a setup on the company's SVD-185 gouge jig to create the same fingernail profile over and over again. The key is it uses the edge of the wheel as a reference point, so a worn, smaller stone is no problem, as long as it is dressed and true. The jig is slid onto the tool rest, which is round. Then the tool rest is moved until two metal disks on the jig are resting on the stone (see **Figure 11-16**). That's all there is to repeating a setup initially dialed in months or years ago. That means maintenance on a gouge is repeatable, which in turn means a great deal less grinding. A guide on the back of the setter tells the user how far the gouge needs to slide into the SVD-185 jig (see **Figure 11-17**), so nothing is left to chance. Repeatability is the key to superior sharpening.

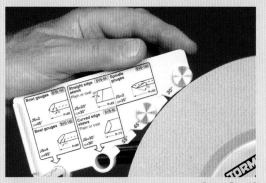

Figure 11-16. To set turning tool angles on a Tormek, lay the plastic jig on the wheel and tighten the tool rest.

Figure 11-15. Cindy Drozda turned the delicate finial on the lid of this vessel using a fingernail gouge that she ground almost to a point. The title of her piece is "Unununium Connundrum."

Figure 11-17. The gouge must have an exact amount of its shaft protruding through the jig.

Figure 11-18. Turners must experiment with sharpening. The two gouges at right have fingernail grinds while the two skews at left have a slightly curved edge.

Skews for turning

There are two kinds of skews, flat and oval. In **Figure 11-18**, both are shown alongside a pair of gouges showing variations on the fingernail grind, with the one on the far left having a longer side grind. The flat and oval skews shown at the right each show a small radius formed using Tormek's SVS-50 jig. Some turners believe the slight arc allows them to travel around a bead or shoulder more smoothly than a straight grind would. One such master turner, Alan Lacer, grinds a more pronounced radius on some of the flat skews he sells, while he eschews oval skews altogether. Other experienced turners swear by them, citing superior strength, smoother movement, and easier grinds (see **Figure 11-19**). Oval skews from the Robert Sorby Company in Sheffield, England, are described as offering "smooth usage and won't cut into the tool rest. [They are] also quite nice for shaping beads and cylinders."

Figure 11-19. Turners differ on whether oval or flat skews work best, but both sharpen easily on a slow wet stone.

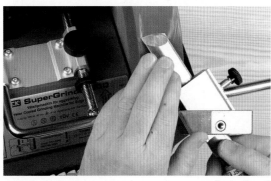

Scrapers

Because they are flat, turning scrapers are quite easy to sharpen. The bevel is shallow, between 70 and 80 degrees, because scrapers need a lot of backup to absorb chatter and impact, and also because they don't need a lot of cutting action. After grinding, turners use a burnisher on the scraper to raise the burr that does the actual cutting.

Straight and round-nose scrapers are most common and other shapes abound, though most are variations of a simple radius. Some scrapers have a small relief a little way back from the edge to help them work around corners. There are several versions with interchangeable heads, and they come with specific sharpening instructions. There are even scrapers made to create the 15-degree angle required for collet chucks. Some scrapers are quite thick, to reduce chatter, but they are all ground at roughly the same 15-degree angle and are burnished whenever possible.

Parting tools

The parting tool completes the starter set. The standard version is used for parting off (separating) work between centers, squaring up the ends of blanks, and cutting tenons for chucks. There is a flat version, and also a diamond shape (where the top and bottom faces each have a ridge). Some people are quite fond of the latter variety, claiming it reduces friction. However, several noted turners are on record as not liking it at all, saying it is hard to sharpen and use. Crown Tools in England makes a thin, wide parting tool. It is about ¹⁄₁₆" thick and has only one angle on the front edge, like a skew.

Step 1. The standard grind on a skew is more predictable than that of most turning tools. Looking at a skew from the side, the edge angles back from the top at 20 to 30 degrees, and the included angle, looking down from the top, can be as steep as 25 degrees. New turners may prefer a larger angle, more like 30 to 35 degrees. The bevel can be ground on a bench grinder with a medium to fine stone (60- to100-grit friable is a good choice).

Step 2. Because the business end of a skew has a pair of compound angles, the setup for grinding requires two different angles. Set the tool rest on your grinder to 12.5 degrees, and then use a jig to present the tool to the stone at 30 degrees. The setup shown here is on a Woodtek slow horizontal grinder. Grinding on a 400-grit stone followed by polishing on a 1,000-grit stone delivers great results. The jig shown is a piece of white oak with a 60-degree angle cut on each side. By clamping it to the center of the long tool rest, both sides of the block can be used, so both sides of the skew can be dressed.

Step 3. The facets could also be ground and honed on a series of bench stones by setting a jig to 12.5 degrees and locking the skew in the jig at 30 degrees. It's slower than using a powered grinder, but just as effective—use aggressive diamond stones in the early stages, and finish on fine water stones. Skews can dig into a stone or wear a groove quickly, so change the pattern of the strokes for uniform wear.

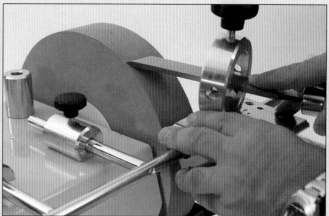

Step 4. Alternately, the entire process can be handled on a vertical grinder, using a jig that allows that 30-degree offset. Some jigs allow for that gentle curve. It's very difficult to grind the arc on bench stones, but with a little practice you can do so on a wheel. Simply sweep the handle end as you work to create the curve.

STEP-BY-STEP: Sharpening a Scraper

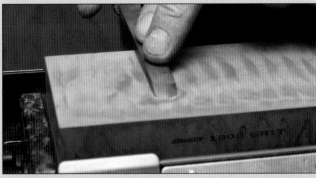

Step 1. Set the tool rest of your grinder at somewhere between 10 and 20 degrees (most commonly 15 degrees), depending on personal preference. Square-ended scrapers (they look like extremely dull bench chisels) are easiest to grind. With a round scraper, hold it against the rest and keep it moving from side to side to maintain a uniform curve. Quench often to avoid heat buildup, and check the angle with a try square.

Step 2. With the leading edge ground, polish the top and bottom faces on a 1,000-grit water stone. Polishing will remove the burr created by the grinder, which would have happened anyway the first time the tool met wood. The grinder burr is uneven, delicate, and leans too far forward to be of use to you.

Step 3. Burnish the top of the ground edge to raise a new burr. As with cabinet scrapers, the goal is to remove thin shavings from the work, not powder. A standard burnishing tool will work, but it's a little awkward. The device shown is the Veritas burnisher, which rolls a hook onto the edge. It comes with two 1"-long carbide rods, one ground at 10 degrees to burnish scrapers from 70 to 75 degrees and the other ground at 5 degrees for scrapers with a bevel from 75 to 80 degrees. The burnisher can be clamped in a vise or screwed to a bench, allowing you to use your entire body for leverage. Because of that, it works with high-speed steel scrapers as well as with carbon steel tools.

Step 4. To change the shape of a scraper to create a specific profile, draw the desired shape on the top face and grind to the line. A long sweep along one side, with a tight radius on the other, is a popular alternative grind.

STEP-BY-STEP: Sharpening a Parting Tool

Step 1. Regrind the edge to the angle you want. For most parting tools, that's in the neighborhood of 35 degrees on each side. Use the tool rest and grind both faces equally. A slight hollow grind produced by the curved edge of the grindstone is perfectly acceptable.

Step 2. You can touch up a parting tool between grindings by using a bench stone, but it's virtually impossible to find a manufactured jig that will hold the tool at the right angle. That leaves building a shop-made jig or honing freehand. Use 1000- and 4000-grit stones to touch up the two ground facets, working both sides equally to maintain the sharp point. Be careful of wobbling or leaning to one side.

Sharpening Sessions: Carving Tools

Knives, Gouges, Bents and Spoons, Chisels and Skews

Carving describes several different types of woodworking. The simplest is traditional chip carving, imported from Europe and perfected over generations on the front porches of Appalachia, and anywhere else where species like basswood, butternut, or cottonwood grow. All that's needed are a few small knives (usually one each for roughing, carving, and detailing), but most chip carvers have a wide selection of personal favorites. Collecting and testing new knives is part of the fun.

The hand tools used in two-dimensional relief carving and three-dimensional wood sculpture are more complicated. Most of them take the form of a chisel, rather than a knife. They share some terminology and profiles with turning tools (gouges and skews), and they also have their own vocabulary (spoons, fishtails, and V-tools).

Common carving tools can be grouped into six types:

- chip carving knives,
- carving gouges,
- bent gouges and spoons,
- V-tools,
- carving chisels and skews, and
- drawknives.

Let's begin with chip carving knives.

Courtesy Woodcraft Supply, LLC

Chip carving knives

Basic tools in the chip carver's arsenal include a large roughing knife, a medium blade, and a small detail knife. Chip carving knives are generally straight, or slightly bowed in shape. Larger blades are thicker than smaller ones. That makes sense because a roughing knife is expected to work harder, so it needs to resist bending or snapping. The tool steel is usually O-1 (an oil-hardened, non-deforming grade that can be hardened at low temperature), or a grade close to it. The knives are generally not too brittle, and they hold an edge well. Shorter blades are a safe and easily controlled choice for new carvers, while experienced chip carvers tend to like longer knives. There are hundreds of knife manufacturers in the United States alone, most of them small, one-man shops that produce custom, handmade tools in an unbelievable variety of shapes (see **Figure 11-20**).

Most chip carving knives can be sharpened on a series of bench stones, following the same simple routine. Begin by applying the cleaner recommended by the stones' manufacturer (oil or water), and allow it to soak in for the required amount of time.

Figure 11-20. Chip carving knives are made in a variety of styles, but most have a short, sharp blade that has one flat side and one side with a primary and a secondary bevel. Photo courtesy Woodcraft Supply LLC.

Step 1. Use a medium-grit stone to establish the bevel. This is somewhere between 25 and 30 degrees, but the exact angle isn't terribly important. What is important is consistency. You must learn to hold the knife at the same angle throughout. If the angle opens or closes as the knife moves away from your body, the edge will be rounded. With curved blades, work the whole edge by moving your hand in a gentle arc without changing the angle.

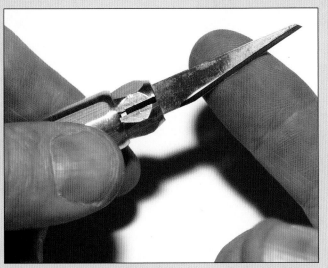

Step 2. For each stone grit, work one face completely, and then turn the blade over to work the other face. You'll know it's time to change when you can feel a uniform burr along the entire length of the back of the edge. This is rolled steel, and it's usually too small to see, but you can feel it with your fingertips. Move your fingers away from the edge (rather than into it) so that you don't cut yourself. Work through a 1000-grit water stone and then a 4000-grit, or the equivalent medium and fine grits in oilstones or diamond stones.

Step 3. Turning the blade over will eliminate the burr from the first face. Remove the burr from the second face by stropping—touching the blade against a charged revolving leather wheel for a couple of seconds to polish it. Maintain the same angle you used while honing on the stones. Test your knife by slicing across (and not into) some pine or fir end grain. It should slice cleanly across the fibers.

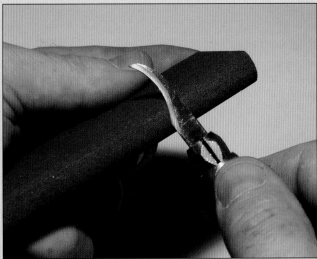

Step 4. Chip carving knives with a concave (hollow) profile can be honed quickly on a series of slips. I find diamond cones work well in the early stages, and oilstone slips do a good job of final honing. Clean up the work area and the tools before switching between grits or between types of stone. A fine stone with coarse grit on it becomes a coarse stone.

Carving gouges

Carving is a very personal form of woodworking. Unlike furniture building or cabinetry, where the same plan can be used ad infinitum by generations of craftsmen, carving is more art than craft. There are standard subjects (a good example is the study of acanthus leaves by Michael Dow, see **Figure 11-21**), but the craft lends itself to individual interpretation and plays of imagination. The same is true of the chisels carvers use. There is a limited set of standard profiles, and innumerable variations of these. When it comes to sharpening, the profiles are gouges, V-tools, flats, and skews, as shown in **Figure 11-22**. Let's begin with straight gouges, and we'll touch on fishtails and other variants in a little while.

It helps to understand the geometry of a gouge. The arc along the cutting edge (called the sweep) can be almost flat, or it can be U-shaped, or usually somewhere in between. Major manufacturers describe the curvature of that arc using a scale that ranges from 1 to 11, where 1 is flat. They also specify the width of the tool. In **Figure 11-23**, the small number to the right of each curve is the measurement, in a straight line, from one tip of the arc to the other. It is expressed as millimeters. Shown here are the #1, #6, and #11 sweeps in the Two Cherries collection.

Courtesy Lee Valley & Veritas

Figure 11-22. Carving tools, even high-quality ones, are shipped a little dull so that a novice won't open the box and be injured.

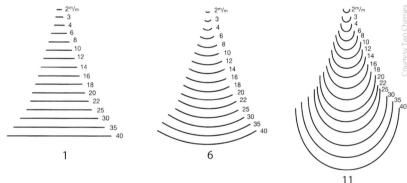

Courtesy Two Cherries

Figure 11-23. Major manufacturers use a standard system for specifying gouges. They measure the width and identify the curvature or sweep on a scale ranging from 1 to 11, where 1 is flat.

Figure 11-21. Acanthus leaves are a standard carving subject, but Michael Dow has interpreted them his own way in this study.

Grinding Wheels for Carving Tools

Most carving tools have only a primary bevel and no secondary bevel. Establish the bevel on a slow grinder, using a white friable 8" aluminum oxide wheel. "Friable" refers to the ability of the abrasive grains to fracture and present new facets to the tool. A wheel stamped with a J or K (a measure of hardness) works well. Make sure the quenching well for the grinder is topped off with cool water before you begin.

Step 1. Set the angle of the tool rest on your grinder. You generally want about a 25-degree bevel for push strokes, and a stouter 30-degree bevel if you'll tap the gouge with a mallet. A single bevel is all you need (no secondary). Begin with a medium wheel (46-to-60 grit) the first time through, and then change to a fine wheel (80-grit).

Step 2. Gently approach the wheel and move the tool from side to side after making contact. To avoid overgrinding the center, move the tool quickly through it. Quench the gouge after each swivel pass. That cool water will keep you from drawing out the temper of the steel. Heat is the enemy.

Step 3. Check often for a uniform burr inside the sweep. When you can feel one all the way across the tool, it's time to switch to a finer stone. After the second grinding, use shaped stones to remove the burr. Called slip stones, the most common are Arkansas oilstones, with diamond-coated slips becoming increasingly common.

Step 4. Use a leather strop to polish both the ground edge and the inside of the sweep. A charged cotton buffing wheel also works. Keep in mind the wheel turns into the tool when grinding, but it must turn away from the edge when buffing or stropping. If you were to feed the new edge into a leather or cotton wheel, it would catch dangerously.

Step 5. Fishtail gouges flare out from the handle to the cutting edge, getting wider as they go. They will fit into tight spots, where regular gouges won't. Sharpening fishtails calls for almost the same process as straight gouges, except they are generally wider and somewhat tapered. Keep the taper in mind as you roll the gouge against the grindstone. To keep the cutting edge square, use a sliding T-bevel to keep track of it.

Step 6. Several manufacturers make special jigs that hold gouges on their slow, wet sharpening systems. The jigs add a great deal of control for wide fishtail gouges. Using the jig, follow the steps outlined above and finish up by stropping or buffing.

Bent gouges and spoons

Some gouges do not have straight shafts. Some have an offset or bent shaft and others have a step, called a drop. These tools aren't often needed, but they can really save the day when a straight shaft won't reach into a crevice or corner. They can be tricky to sharpen without a jig, but become quite manageable with the right attachment. Tormek, along with other manufacturers, offers a special jig for the unusually shaped tools (see **Figure 11-24**).

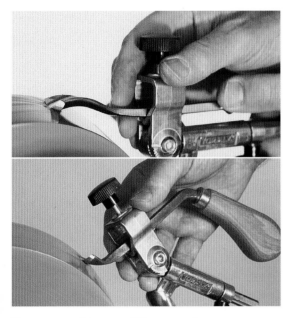

Figure 11-24. Two very different carving gouges can be sharpened using the same jig (the SVD-185) on a Tormek 2000.

V-Tools

Sometimes called a parting tool, a carver's V-tool is L-shaped, like an angle iron. Rotate it 45 degrees and it becomes a V. The bevels are on the two outside faces, which can simplify sharpening. There are variations to the angle of the V that run from a small 45 degrees to a wide 100 degrees and beyond, and the sides of some flare like a bird's wings, but most are close to 90 degrees. It's possible to sharpen V-tools on a vertical

Courtesy Wood Artistry, L.L.C.

Figure 11-25. A 20- to 25-degree bevel can be formed on straight V-tool using a horizontal grinder or a bench stone.

grindstone, but you'll achieve better results on a slow horizontal grinder (see **Figure 11-25**) so there is no hollow grind. The angle of the bevel varies according to taste, but 20 degrees is a good place to start. This draws a long bevel, and the steel becomes thin. If you'll use a mallet, add another 5 degrees to strengthen the bevel.

Carving chisels and skews

Carving chisels, like standard bench chisels, have a squared end. Unlike bench chisels, they have two bevels (see **Figure 11-26**), which means they don't take off in one direction, but go where they are sent with the tap of a mallet.

Figure 11-26. Carving chisels have squared ends, the same as bench chisels, but have two bevels instead of one, making it possible to steer them in the wood.

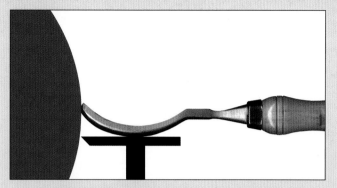

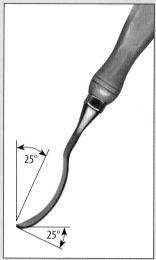

Step 2. Swivel the handle slightly from side to side, checking frequently the grind is uniform across the entire cutting edge. To check that it is, hold the tool at about 25 degrees, and look straight down at the tip of the blade. It will be straight across, or nearly so. Quench the tool every few seconds to keep it cool. As you gain experience, you may want to grind a sharper bevel (all the way to 45 degrees, depending on the work).

Step 1. Sharpening without a jig begins with setting the angle of the grinder's tool rest. The goal is to grind a bevel at about 25 degrees. For most tools, the rest would be set at 65 degrees, but the bent shaft changes it. A standard setting would force you to hold the chisel well below the wheel's axis. Setting the tool rest only slightly below the axis and locking it level works for many bent gouges, and allows you to see what's happening.

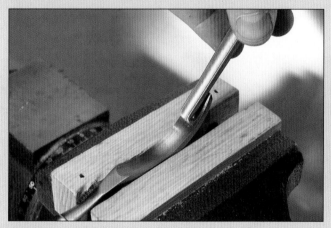

Step 3. When you have raised a burr all of the way across the cutting edge, you are done grinding. Remove the burr with a cone-shaped or cylindrical slip. This can be difficult to do with a curved shaft. Work within ¼" or so of the edge so the curve doesn't force the slip to create a new bevel on the inside of the sweep.

Step 4. Strop both sides of the bevel, polishing the grind on the outside and removing any residual burr on the inside.

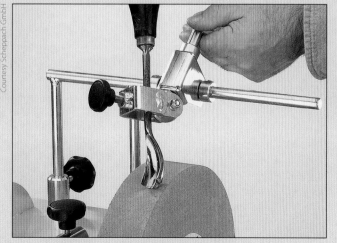

Step 5. Spoons are a cross between a fishtail and a bent gouge. They have a deep cavity just behind the edge that allows them to scoop into recesses. This makes them ideal for relieving deep backgrounds and reaching behind wings, arms, and other obstacles in sculpture. They can be sharpened the same as other bent gouges, although it's a whole lot easier to secure them in a jig such as the Scheppach model shown here.

Step 1. I like to establish the bevel on a coarse diamond stone to save some time. That means locking the V-tool into a honing guide. Most guides won't handle a tool this thick, but the least expensive one on the market does. Note the flat side of the V-tool rests against the flat edge of the guide, while the tapered side sits tightly against the curved edge. Set the guide for a 20-degree bevel, and then work both outside faces equally. Feel for a burr, and use a small diamond file to remove it after it forms all the way across both edges.

Step 2. Keeping the tool in the jig, move to a 1,000-grit water stone or the equivalent to refine the bevel. Being able to use a simple jig on a flat bench stone is a luxury with carving tools, so take advantage of the situation to hone a perfect bevel. Note the small yellow mark on the shaft of the tool. That is a registration mark for placing the tool in the jig at exactly the same spot after switching to the other face.

Step 3. Stay with the bench stones and, after forming and removing a burr, move to an 8,000-grit abrasive. The very fine stone will almost polish the bevel while removing most of the scratches from the earlier abrasives. Work both outside faces to raise a final burr. You'll also notice a small tail has formed where the two walls of the V-tool meet. The tail is the accumulation of the two burrs, and it needs to be removed or the tool will use it as a kind of rudder to steer across wood in directions other than the one you choose.

Step 4. Use small slips to remove the final burrs. The diamond file is a bit coarse, and it won't reach all the way into the corner. Follow up by stropping all four faces (bevels and backs), and test the tool by carving a shallow groove across the grain of some pine.

Step 1. If you need to establish the bevel, set the grinder tool rest for 20 degrees and grind a new bevel on each side of the tool. Quench often to avert heat buildup, and make sure the bevels are equal so the point is centered in the tool's shaft.

Step 2. Lock the chisel into a honing guide at 20 degrees and soak a medium-grit (1,000) water stone. Fill your spray bottle with water. It's essential to keep the stone wet to wash away small metal particles, or they will clog the stone's pores and create a glaze.

Step 3. Work the chisel on the medium stone until you have raised a small burr along the back of the edge. You can feel it with your fingertips and see it under magnification. The burr must extend all of the way across the edge. Remove the tool from the jig, turn it over, and reinstall it. Then work the second bevel. That will remove the first burr and begin raising a second one.

Step 4. When the second burr extends all the way across the blade, switch to a 4,000-grit stone. The initial couple of passes will remove the second burr and begin a new one. Work both faces until the 4,000-grit stone has raised a burr on the edge along the second face, and then go to the 8,000-grit stone.

Step 5. Remove this final burr and polish both bevels on a charged leather strop or a cloth buff. The most effective method is a slow-moving leather wheel (200-300 rpm) chucked in the drill press, although any strip of fine leather will work. Keep the angle of address (the point where the tool meets the strop) at 20 degrees, or a hair less. If you go over 20 degrees, you'll round your new, crisp cutting edge.

Step 6. Sharpening a double-beveled skew is exactly the same as sharpening a straight carving chisel, except that you lock the chisel into the jig at the skew angle (usually between 10 degrees and 20 degrees). Carvers' skews can be right-beveled, left-beveled, or double-beveled. As with most carving tools, they come in several sizes: The photo shows a full-size right skew and a double-beveled, miniature palm skew. Some carvers like to grind a small arc along the cutting edges of their skews. The arc helps make curved cuts around flowers and leaves.

Drawknives

Rarely seen anymore in the average woodshop, drawknives once were a staple in the arsenals of carpenters, cabinetmakers, wheelwrights, coopers, and a myriad of other trades. They still find a home with boat builders, willow furniture makers, log house builders, and other specialty craftsmen, particularly those who work with green (unseasoned) wood. They can be pulled (the usual method) or pushed, and are ideal for removing bark from logs, or the thinnest sliver from a convex curve. The handles can be offset (higher than the blade), or at the same height. The blade can be straight or slightly curved.

Drawknives work well with a chisel grind of 25 to 30 degrees. The bevel can be formed on a machine (preferable), or by hand. On a machine, use a jig to pass the edge across a wide wheel (see **Figure 11-27**), and follow the manufacturer's instructions.

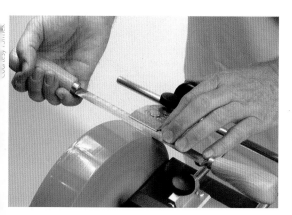

Figure 11-27. Long, thin cutters such as drawknives are difficult to sharpen successfully on anything but a slow wet wheel.

Sharpening by hand requires locking the knife in a vise and working the edge with a series of bench stones while trying to maintain exactly the same bevel angle through several stone grits. Hand sharpening is not an experience I would recommend to new woodworkers, because it can be quite frustrating, but old hands favor it. Some even use files. Follow the machine stage with a stropping, which also is the way to maintain the bevel during use (see **Figure 11-28**).

Courtesy Tormek®

Figure 11-28. When stropping drawknives, the top of the leather wheel must be traveling away from the edge or it will dig in.

Inshaves and scorps

An inshave has a similar purpose to a drawknife, only it comes at the work from a different angle. Think of a drawknife that has been bent almost all of the way into a circle. The inshave also requires a chisel grind. Several manufacturers have created jigs to handle the awkward tools, as shown in **Figure 11-29**. Sharpen the one-handled version of the inshave, called a scorp, in exactly the same way (see **Figure 11-30**).

Rotate the tool into the stone at a steady rate to create a uniform bevel around the entire edge. Both benefit from a quick stropping. And both are frustrating to work on a standard bench grinder. It's probably smarter to clamp them in a vise and sharpen them with diamond bench stones if a slow wet grinder isn't available. In that case, swipe the stones across the bevel, rather than up and down, to keep from cutting yourself.

Courtesy Tormek®

Figure 11-29. A large platen, such as the face of Tormek's SVD-110 jig, is essential to support inshaves and maintain the angle.

Courtesy Tormek®

Figure 11-30. Scorps are easier to sharpen than you might think because the bevel is on the outside where it can contact the stone.

Sharpening Sessions: Mattocks

Adzes, Axes, and Hatchets

Though rarely found in a modern woodworking shop, adzes and axes once were basic carpentry tools. The general name for this class of tool is "mattocks." A few boat builders and carvers still use them, but powered carving tools (and the occasional chainsaw) have largely replaced them. They're more popular now as firewood generators than as woodworking tools (see **Figure 11-31**). Given their centuries of service, they still deserve respect.

Figure 11-31. Adzes and axes, once common in the woodworking shop, nowadays generate mostly firewood. They do their best work when sharp.

Despite their size, flat adzes and axes are quite easy to sharpen. They usually require only grinding, and sometimes a very quick honing. They rely more heavily on speed, force, and the power of impact than on a slicing or cutting action. A hatchet is a short-handled axe, often with a hammer on the back end of the head. It can be sharpened in the same manner as any other axe. Let's touch briefly on maintaining an edge on these large lumber cutters, just in case you ever need to sharpen one.

Adzes

Adzes are ancient tools, used to transform the rough face of lumber to a smooth, curved finish. They are long handled (like an axe), and the normal way to use them is to stand on the work, or with one foot on either side, and swing the adze down to a stop between the feet. After each stroke, step backward a little and swing again. The adze will chop or slice, depending on the grain direction and the shape and the sharpness of the leading edge. The blade is perpendicular to the handle. Craftsman recreating historic ships, along with those living in less-industrialized countries, tend to be the main users of the adze. Electric planes have largely taken their place in more developed areas, except in rare trades such as cooperage and some wood sculpture.

Axes and hatchets

Axes and hatchets often are used outdoors where a bench grinder isn't available. You might be splitting firewood or harvesting wood in a forest, bringing home a Christmas tree, or installing a split-rail fence around a pasture. A coarse diamond-coated bench stone is small enough to go to the job site, and aggressive enough to grind an edge in a few strokes (see **Figure 11-32**). It isn't as uniform as a grindstone, but it's a lot easier to haul into the woods. Merely swipe the blade back and forth several times on each face. No water is required, but if there's a stream handy . . .

When you do return to the workshop, take the time to tune up your axe and make it ready for your next woods excursion.

Figure 11-32. To field sharpen an axe, use the aggressive cutting power of a rough diamond sharpener.

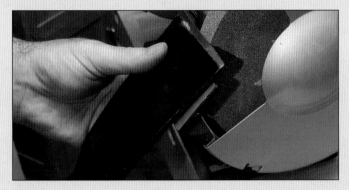

Step 1. The edge of a mattock-type tool must be keen and beveled, but oversharpening just invites the fine edge to shatter or degrade upon impact. An adze usually absorbs less force than an axe (it's a shorter swing), so it can carry a better edge. Most people grind an adze at 20 degrees on each side. For dense hardwoods, go a little higher (15 degrees or so on each side).

Step 2. Grinding on a coarse- and then a medium-grit abrasive will deliver good results. A 36-grit gray wheel will remove steel in a hurry and reveal the bevels. Follow up on an 80-grit wheel to clean up the edges. The blade of a flat adze is wider than most grinder wheels, so you must move it from side to side to maintain a uniform bevel. You'll have to use the rest because there are no commercial jigs big enough to control such a large tool.

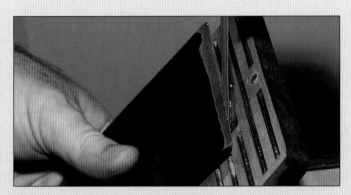

Step 3. Another option is to use a 1" belt sander. With a 30" or longer belt, heat buildup usually isn't a problem. Install a coarse belt to start (60-grit) and follow up with a medium one (100-grit). Even with this much steel to absorb heat, it's a good idea to dip the head in a bucket of water every few seconds to keep it cool. Losing the temper in a tool that absorbs strong impacts is not a great idea. Complete the job with some 180-grit wet/dry paper and a sanding block, always maintaining the angle.

Step 4. A curved adze (sometimes called a bowl adze or a carver's adze) requires more patience than a straight one, and more awareness of its angle with the wheel or stone. The bevel is on the inside and is difficult to reach. One surprisingly successful method is to use a large drum sander chucked in a drill press, or an oscillating drum sander, and work down through the grits to fine.

Step 5. Lipped adzes (also referred to as shipwrights' adzes) have a small upturn on each side called a lip. These must be sharpened, too, because their function is to separate fibers when you work the adze across the grain, rather than along it. Round files, coarse diamond files, and slip stones work well to access the small, curved bevels.

Step 6. Rust is a problem with some mattocks, in part because we often store them outside, but also because of the varied quality of their steel. After a workout, coat these large blades with a light mist of oil (WD-40 works fine), and then slip a plastic bag over the head. Secure it with a rubber band, and it will keep rust at bay.

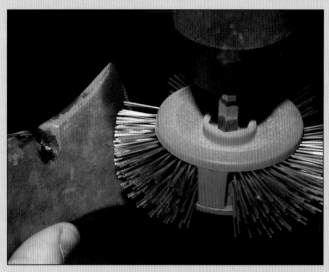

Step 1. If rust has built up on the axe, remove it on a motorized wire brush. Rust pits along the bevel can weaken the steel. Heavy rust also can hide a stress fracture, which is not at all common (but not unknown), and which can be quite dangerous. In maritime locations, rust has a ferocious appetite and can play havoc with small hatchets and axes.

Step 2. A two-sided axe should be ground at 10 degrees on each side, and a little more for hardwoods (12 to 15 degrees). Set the tool rest to 10 degrees and use a coarse stone to establish the bevel on each side. A 1" long-belt sander is a viable option (see Adzes, Step 3, on page 117).

Courtesy Scheppach GmbH

Step 3. Some axes have a pronounced curve to the cutting edge. The curved edge is intended for green wood. The curve allows wet fibers to slide to the side and be sliced. Many wet stones have jigs that will accommodate smaller axes, especially those with a bevel on each side. Using the center of the head as a pivot point, they swing an arc to maintain the curve.

Sharpening Sessions: Machine Cutters

Planer Knives, Shaper Knives, Router Bits, Circular Saw Blades

Machine cutters take a terrific pounding as they whirl through woods of every texture and hardness. Because of the hard work they do, they're usually made of extremely tough steel or are tipped with super-hard alloys like tungsten carbide. And because of the amount of work they do, they quickly become coated with hardened deposits of pitch and resin that interfere with their cutting geometry.

The first step in restoring a machine cutter is to remove the gunk by soaking the cutter in a commercial gum and pitch remover, or in a solvent such as lacquer thinner. However, the volatile solution should only be used outdoors, where its noxious and flammable fumes can't hurt your lungs or reach the pilot light on the furnace. An old pizza pan makes a nice bath, and a layer of Clingwrap® over the top will minimize fumes and evaporation. After a half-hour soak, a brass bristle brush will remove the softened residue that remains.

Planer knives

Planers are the hardest working machines in the shop. They are continuously asked to remove huge quantities of material across the entire width of a board. Few of the knives are carbide, and we're asking a lot of high-speed steel (HSS) here, especially if the cutting edges must conquer figure, knots, or other imperfections in the stock being milled. In recent years, portable planers have dramatically increased their market share. Portable is a subjective word: Paul Bunyan would have a job hefting some of these machines. And disposable is debatable, too. The knives can be touched up a couple of times before they must be discarded. Unplug the machine and then remove the knives, following the instructions in its manual. On most portable machines, the cutterhead locks and a cover may then be removed. After that, the knives can be unlocked with an Allen wrench that loosens three or four bolts (see **Figure 11-33**) and then can be lifted out. It's a good idea to use a magnet. The knives may be dull, but they're still sharp enough to slice a finger.

The heavier knives in most stationary planers are held in their pockets by a chipbreaking bar that's retained by a number of locking bolts. Usually you need a small wrench to loosen the bolts. Some machines also have jackscrews for lifting the knives out of their pockets, and also for finely adjusting their height after sharpening and reinstalling. Get in the habit of unplugging the machine or throwing its circuit breaker before you dive inside with wrenches in your bare hands. The last thing you want is an accidental startup from bumping the ON switch while you work.

A jig on a sharpening machine is really the only sensible option because hand sharpening three (or even two) wide knives and hoping they remain identical is a long shot. Many shops send out jointer and planer knives for sharpening. A professional sharpener also will balance the knives to minimize vibration. He or she takes a tiny bit of material off one or both ends of the heaviest knife.

Figure 11-33. To touch up the knives in a portable planer, unplug the machine and remove the cover that holds them in place.

Step 1. Clean the knives, if needed. After several hours of use, especially on pine or similar sap-laden species, a buildup of hardened resins can occur. Buildup also happens when you plane boards that had varnish on them. Resins don't like lacquer thinner, and an overnight soaking will soften them.

Step 2. A jig or dedicated machine is essential for sharpening wide blades. There is no way to do them freehand. Several companies offer jigs for the task (the Scheppach is shown), and even though they take a few minutes to set up, they do an excellent job. Disposable blades offer an inexpensive opportunity to practice sharpening. If the blade suffers during the process, it has already served you well.

Step 3. If a set of knives has been nicked by a nail or a hard knot, try sliding one of the knives to the left, a second to the right, and if there's a third, leave it in the center. By moving the nicks out of line, you can get a decent cut with no evidence of the nick. However, the dodge only works once.

Step 4. On heavier planers and jointers (usually 220 volt or 3-phase), the blades are thicker, are made of better-quality steel, and are intended to be sharpened. Jigs establish the angle for the primary bevel, and you rarely hone any secondary bevel on such wide blades. However, some experienced woodworkers do grind a small back bevel on them for milling hard stock or highly figured grain.

Step 5. Jointer knives can be touched up in place, using a simple jig like the one shown, which is from Rockler Woodworking and Hardware. When that solution fails, they can be sharpened on wet wheels, just like planer knives.

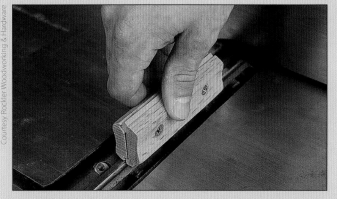

Shaper and molder knives

Molders use flat knives locked into a doughnut-shaped cutterhead to create profiled edges. Shapers use round cutters that drop onto an arbor. Both types are sharpened by dressing their flat faces, rather than working their bevels (as one would with, say, a bench chisel). Begin the process by removing any resin buildup. A bath in lacquer thinner works well, but leave it outdoors because of the fumes. After half an hour or so, any accumulation should be soft enough to remove with a brass wire brush.

Router bits

Router bits are either high-speed steel, carbide, or carbide tipped. The thing to remember is you sharpen only the face that meets the work and never the outside (trailing edge) of the profile. If the bit isn't sharp, it will be hard to push through wood (especially dense hardwoods), and it will burn the wood.

Start by soaking router bits in lacquer thinner for at least 30 minutes (do so outdoors because of the fumes), and then clean them with a brass wire brush, as shown in **Figure 11-34**. On carbide bits, it might be all you need to do because carbide doesn't dull very quickly, but it does accumulate resins, especially when cutting man-made sheet goods such as plywood and MDF.

Circular saw blades

Given the complex geometry of carbide-tipped circular blades, your best option probably is to send them out to a professional sharpening shop. With the array of angles, shapes, gullets, bevels, and carbide quality, you need a certain amount of expertise to work on expensive tools. Fortunately,

Courtesy DMT®, Diamond Machining Technology

Figure 11-35. The new generation of diamond files is ideally suited to lightly touching up the faces of carbide-tipped saw blades.

most problems with carbide tips are not related to dullness. They are the product of buildup, created by resins, glues, sap, and heat. A good 30-minute soaking in a bath of lacquer thinner (don't breathe the fumes!) and a subsequent scrubbing in warm water and soap will restore most carbide-tipped blades. If a small touchup is still required, use a flat diamond sharpener (see **Figure 11-35**) and rub it across the faces only. Don't touch the trailing bevel or the top or sides of the carbide tip, or you'll alter the geometry and diminish its effectiveness.

Figure 11-34. Clean hardened resins off router bits by soaking in lacquer thinner and scrubbing with a brass wire brush. On a carbide bit, cleaning as described might be all you need to do.

Courtesy DMT®, Diamond Machining Technology

Step 1. The quickest way to dress a HSS or carbide molder knife is to lay it flat on a series of diamond bench stones. Slide the cutter back and forth across each stone, working down through the grits from the coarsest to the finest. Use water as a cleaner to keep residue from clogging the stones.

Step 2. Carbide shaper cutters are no more complicated than molder knives. They also have a flat face you can dress with diamond sharpeners. The only difference is the cutters are larger, more three-dimensional, and thus more cumbersome. Some of them won't fit on a flat bench stone, but slim diamond files can solve the problem.

Step 3. Clamp the cutter in a vise with wooden jaws to protect it. Carbide, though hard, is brittle. Dress each face of the cutter (most have two or three) with a series of diamond files, working down through the grits to the finest. Be careful not to change the profile, or the angle at which the cutter meets the work. The carbide inserts are of uniform thickness and should remain so after you have finished. It only takes a few passes to dress them. If you use water to keep the diamond sharpener clean, be sure to dry the cutters thoroughly.

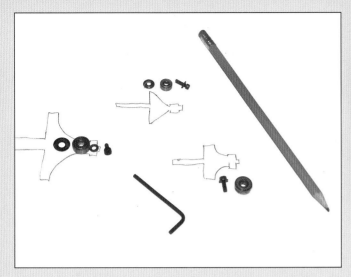

Step 1. Remove the guide bearings. These will get in the way when you try to work the cutting faces. If you're sharpening more than one bit, keep track of the bearings so you can replace them on the correct bits, or you'll change the profiles you cut. One way to do it is to trace the bit on paper and then tape the bearing to the outline.

Step 2. Work down through the grits on diamond bench stones. Nothing else will sharpen carbide. Begin by using a permanent marker to coat the surface to be honed, and then work until the marking disappears, which will tell you when to move to the next finer grade.

Step 3. If the bit won't fit on a bench stone, clamp it in a vise and work the surface with diamond files. Good lighting is essential so you can watch the progress indicated by the disappearing marker ink.

Sharpening Specialty Bits

The only difference between honing a flat tool and a curved one is coping with the shape. All of the principles are the same. One still works from the coarsest abrasive to the finest available. The object is to protect the shape of the cutter while dressing only the edge that meets the work. On a multi-spur bit, that means sharpening the fronts of the teeth (see **Figure 1**). The quickest way to handle it is with a heavy-duty cutoff disk chucked in a rotary tool (such as a Dremel). If that's not available, an old-fashioned fine file works. Be careful not to change the rake (the angle at which the cutting face is sloped back from 90 degrees). If your bit has an open shave (a chisel-shaped blade for clearing out the waste), it can be touched up on the flat side with a diamond file (see **Figure 2**).

A conical drill-mounted grindstone works well to contour and dress the inside edge of a Forstner bit (see **Figure 3**), and they come in lots of sizes to fit any bit. A diamond hone makes short work of touching up the open shave and the center pin (see **Figure 4**).

Run spade bits through a motorized wire wheel to remove rust and buildup of resins, glues, or tar (pitch). Touch up the point and spurs with a heavy-duty cutoff disk in a rotary tool (see **Figure 5**), making sure you only dress the sides of the point. On most spade bits, flattening the faces on a lapping plate helps to re-establish the cutting edge. However, some spade bits have a relief cut into the leading face, and flattening the face of such a bit would actually dull it. Use an old-fashioned file to touch up any sharp edges that can't be reached with the rotary tool. The edges on many flat files have teeth for reaching small spots (see **Figure 6**).

Nothing works more quickly than a diamond slip to touch up the curved inside edges of a hollow mortising chisel (see **Figure 7**). Be sure to stay away from the outside edges of the tool, or you'll change its dimensions. Use the rotary tool's cutoff disk to touch up the cutting edges of the bit that runs inside the chisel. Again, work only the inside faces—the outside dimensions of the bit must remain unchanged (see **Figure 8**).

Figure 1. Sharpen the fronts of the teeth on a multi-spur bit.

Figure 2. Touch up the open shave with a flat diamond file.

Figure 3. Sharpen the inside rim of a Forstner bit with a conical grindstone mounted in a drill.

Figure 4. The flat diamond file touches up the center pin inside a Forstner bit.

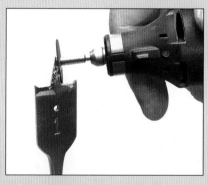
Figure 5. Dress the point and spurs of a spade bit with the rotary cutoff wheel.

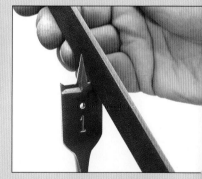
Figure 6. An old-style steel file can reach where the rotary wheel can't.

Figure 7. A diamond slip makes short work of the inside edges on a hollow mortising chisel.

Figure 8. The rotary cutoff disk sharpens the inside faces of the hollow chisel's auger bit.

On files and handsaws

For centuries, the only way to sharpen saws and similar hand tools was with a series of files (see **Figure 11-36**). The sharp, multi-faceted instruments are forged from the hardest and most brittle steel. Today, files are rapidly being replaced in the world of sharpening by harder, more efficient diamond hones. As woodworking tools, files and rasps still play a vital role, but as sharpening agents, their role is being usurped by diamond files and by ceramic files that use metal as a base so they can be manufactured in virtually any shape. You'll still find a few occasions for using old-fashioned files, such as sharpening a chainsaw with a rat-tail file. But in general, files are becoming as dated as a hand-cranked grindstone.

Handsaws, too, have largely seen their day, being replaced by the power and speed of electric motors. A few have survived for special needs such as dovetailing and veneer work. While they are a joy to use, not one of the professional woodworkers I questioned ever has felt the need to sharpen them, as they see such infrequent use. In truth, the value of handsaws today seems to be more nostalgic than practical.

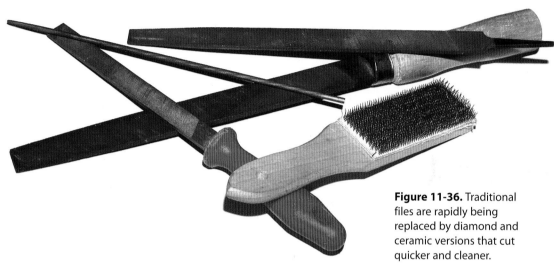

Figure 11-36. Traditional files are rapidly being replaced by diamond and ceramic versions that cut quicker and cleaner.

Restoring Handsaws

For craftsmen who would like to try restoring a handsaw, I'd suggest a virtual visit to Pete Taran's place. Pete is an associate editor of the Fine Tool Journal, and he runs the Vintage Saws website. He gives a very detailed online class in sharpening and setting handsaws, and sells refurbished saws that have been expertly serviced. He pioneered the return of the high-quality Western dovetail saw in 1996, and sold that business to Lie-Nielsen in 1998. Pete invites you to visit vintagesaws.com and peruse his library.

CHAPTER 12

Sharpening Stations

A sharpening station can be as simple or as complex as the woodworking it supports. In Japan, woodworkers have traditionally knelt on the floor, leaning over nothing more than a set of water stones. Americans like to stand up, have one or two machines available, and keep a couple of drawers handy to hold bench stones and other equipment.

One of the most fascinating things about sharpening is some of the best carvers, turners, and furniture builders have very simple setups that are efficient. A lifetime of experience has refined the options for them. Even those who have very elaborate sharpening setups gravitate to just a few options when it comes time to work.

Designing your sharpening station

The format of a sharpening station really depends on the type of work you are doing. For turners, a slow-speed grinder is a given, whether it's a wet or dry machine. Turners and carvers need to strop, and for carvers, a selection of shaped slip stones, usually pocket-sized, sees a lot of use. For woodworkers who build cabinetry or furniture, bench stones are essential.

When planning a sharpening center, there are several general guidelines to bear in mind. These have emerged from speaking with a number of serious woodworkers about the subject. The guidelines are as follows:

- Many turners suggest the center of a grindstone should be around the same height as the chuck on a lathe. That's a subjective guideline because some people like the chuck at elbow height, while others prefer something a bit lower. Either way, the grindstone definitely should be mounted as close to the lathe as possible, without interfering with the work.
- For people working with bench stones, the Japanese model has merit. Being able to position your body over the stone gives you more leverage, and hence more control over the action. The relationship between leverage and control suggests the stone should be secured on a surface a few inches lower than a workbench.
- Bench stones and lapping plates need to be trapped on the work surface so they can't move around. Wooden guide strips are a good solution. Some angle jig designs need stone-thickness rails on which to roll; usually they can be built into the stone-trapping system.
- Sharpening is messy, no matter what technology you adopt. Grinders produce piles of black abrasive dust; oilstones can leave an oily mess you do not want to transfer onto your clean wood; water stones make mud and the action of sharpening causes it to slosh around. So design for that—sharpen away from your workbench, and make your station from materials that clean up easily.
- Along with the sharpening equipment you use every day, provide storage space for the sharpening equipment you no longer use, or think you might need someday, or don't (yet) know how to use. You'd be amazed by how much sharpening stuff a pack-rat personality can accumulate.

However one decides to set up, and whatever is included, perhaps the best way to glean ideas for a sharpening center is to peek into the shops of some of America's most innovative woodworkers. Throughout the following tour, each woodworker's own comments are included whenever possible. The author and the publisher are grateful to the busy and generous people for their information, their photographs, and their time.

Chris Billman, woodworker

Chris Billman's extremely well-organized sharpening center has, well, everything (see **Figure 12-1**). Billman, an amateur woodworker who lives in Ypsilanti Township, Michigan, builds furniture for his family and has dabbled in turning (see **Figures 12-2** and **12-3**). He is involved with several philanthropic organizations including Toys for Tots and the Freedom Pens project.

His sharpening setup began with a couple of sturdy beech cabinets salvaged from a community college lab. The eight drawers offer plenty of dust-free storage, and the cabinets are just the right height for the type of sharpening he or she enjoys doing. On the countertops, the equipment is laid out in a logical manner, with machines at the back and room for bench stones up front. He installed a desk lamp at the far left, knowing good light means good work.

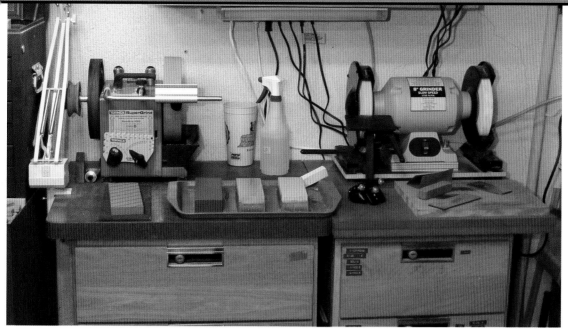

Courtesy Chris Billman

Here's how Chris Billman describes his sharpening center:

"This has evolved over the last few years. It started with a dedicated corner of my bench for the Tormek. I added a 6" variable-speed bench grinder and a few more stones and devoted a single base cabinet to sharpening. When I replaced the 6" grinder with an 8" Woodcraft slow-speed bench grinder and a Oneway Wolverine system for turning tools, I expanded the area to two base cabinets and part of a wall cabinet (not shown). The grinders rest permanently on the work surfaces, ready to go at a moment's notice. All of the jigs, stones, and other necessary sharpening paraphernalia are stored in the cabinets. I think I have too much sharpening stuff . . .

"What a luxury to have everything centralized! It's still a chore to sharpen a tool, but it's much less of a drudgery because there's a dedicated space with everything I need. It seems I'm now less prone to postponing maintenance sharpening. I often make the trip to the grinder or stones to give an edge tool a quick touchup and get right back to work. It's well worth a few square feet of shop space.

"In the picture, you can see (from left to right) the Norton flattening stone I use to keep the

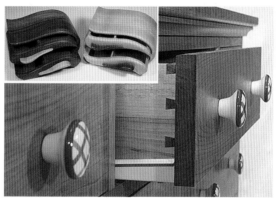

Courtesy Chris Billman

Figure 12-2. Chris Billman is a serious wood hobbyist, and the quality of his work matches the high standards of his sharpening.

stones flat during usage—an 800-grit stone, a 4,000-grit stone, and a King 8,000-grit stone. You'll also notice a small Nagura stone in the upper right corner of the water tray, the spray bottle of water (to keep the stones wet) above the tray, and the Veritas Mark II honing jig to the right of the tray. For most touchup sharpening tasks, I skip the 800-grit stone. I keep an MDF cutoff loaded with green honing compound for final stropping of tools after the 8,000-grit stone. The 800-grit stone rests immersed in water in a plastic container, and the other stones are flattened, and then dried and stored."

Billman's slow-speed bench grinder (1,725 rpm) creates less heat, and the wheels are 8" in diameter (as opposed to the standard 6"). That means his tools have a very slight hollow grind. By the way, his entire shop is just as beautifully laid out and organized as his sharpening center.

Courtesy Chris Billman

Figure 12-3. Chris Billman.

Figure 12-4. James Krenov has spent a lifetime distilling cabinetry to its very essence and his sharpening regimen reflects it.

James Krenov, cabinetmaker

Internationally renowned, James Krenov is the author of several groundbreaking books on cabinetry and woodworking. He created and led the Fine Woodworking School at the College of the Redwoods in Fort Bragg, California, for 20 years, while continuing to build his own fine cabinets. His work is on museum display in Sweden, Norway, Japan, and the United States. He retired from the college in 2002.

One might expect Krenov to have a large sharpening center with every piece of equipment imaginable. But Krenov uses a simple regimen limited to three select items, as shown in **Figure 12-4**. They include, he told me, "a carborundum bench stone, a piece of Japanese clay (an oilstone made in Japan), and a small piece of ceramic. I use kerosene on all three and have never had any problems. I keep all three in a pocket at the end of the bench."

Such a simplified approach to sharpening indicates how Krenov regards all aspects of woodworking, especially design. Krenov's cabinetry is delicate, strong, and spiritual, and his craftsmanship is of the first order. Krenov's body of work, like that of Frank Lloyd Wright, Sam Maloof, and Gustav Stickley, is a cornerstone of American artistry. His book titles are *A Cabinetmaker's Notebook*, *With Wakened Hands*, *The Fine Art of Cabinetmaking*, *Worker in Wood*, and *The Impractical Cabinetmaker* (see **Figure 12-5**).

Figure 12-5. James Krenov is the author of five highly regarded books about cabinetmaking.

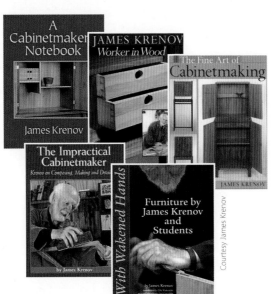

Cindy Drozda, woodturner

One of America's premier turners, Cindy Drozda's work (see **Figure 12-6**) has been featured in most of the popular woodturning magazines both here and abroad. Her studio in Boulder, Colorado, looks out over the front range of the Rockies. Her work has been exhibited in such venues as the Messler Gallery and the Smithsonian Craft Show, among others (see **Figure 12-7**). Drozda was a Niche Award finalist in 2004 and winner of that coveted prize in 2003. A devoted teacher and a generous soul, she reaches out to others in her field in a manner that honors the best traditions of woodworking.

"Keeping the tools sharp is the key to making clean cuts," Drozda says. "We have four sharpening stations in our two-person shop, and although a 6" grinder is shown in the photograph, I now have an 8" model (see Figure 12-6).

"When I learned to accurately grind the bevel angle on the cutting edge of my gouges, my turning improved a lot. The bevel angle and edge shape I choose to use are well-suited to the type of turning I do. I am not suggesting this is the 'correct' tool grind, only that it works well for me. My gouge work consists mainly of either shaping the outsides of hollow vessels with a bowl gouge or finial turning with a spindle gouge. I am using a 40-degree bevel angle on both bowl and spindle gouges, as well as on my roughing gouge. The bevel angle requires low cutting force and gives a clean cut without being difficult to control.

"The roughing gouge is sharpened straight across the flutes, with no wing sweep. My bowl gouges and spindle gouges usually have the wings swept back. I like a parabolic flute shape and a wing ground to a very slight crown. The tip is shaped to different radii, depending upon what job I plan to use a particular tool for. To make smoother concave shapes, I grind away the heel of the gouge, leaving a bevel width at the tip of between $\frac{1}{32}$" and $\frac{3}{16}$", depending on the size of the tool and what job it will be doing."

Drozda has released a DVD, *Elegant Finials* (see **Figure 12-8**), in which she explains in detail her custom approach to sharpening turning tools.

Courtesy Cindy Drozda

Figure 12-7. Three elegant turnings by Cindy Drozda.

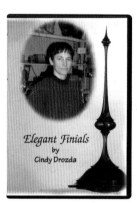

Courtesy Cindy Drozda

Figure 12-8. A DVD produced by master turner Cindy Drozda teaches a special way of sharpening gouges for her delicate, minute finials.

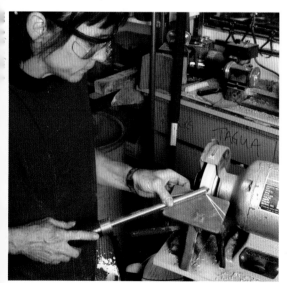

Figure 12-6. Cindy Drozda sharpens a spindle gouge in her studio near Boulder, Colorado.

Figure 12-9. Everett Ellenwood carved this lovely rocking horse for his grandchildren.

Everett Ellenwood, carver

Everett Ellenwood of Rochester, Minnesota, is a master woodcarver with more than 30 years of experience in the workshop and 20 years of teaching; you can see an example of his work in **Figure 12-9**. Ellenwood, the author of a DVD entitled *Sharpening Simplified* and a forthcoming book about woodcarving, has definite views about sharpening carving tools:

"If you look through carving catalogs, you will find a number of sharpening jigs and devices advertised to do wondrous things to assist you in sharpening your tools. If you develop good sharpening techniques, you don't need sharpening jigs. In many cases, it will take more time to attach and position the sharpening jig than it will to get your tools sharp without it.

"There are various types of power sharpeners available to sharpen carving tools. However, from my many years of carving and teaching, I find the majority of tools that are poorly shaped have consistently been sharpened using power sharpeners. I believe strongly that all carvers should learn how to sharpen their tools by hand and learn what the properly sharpened tool should look and feel like. Then, if you want to use power sharpeners, that's up to you. But once a tool is properly contoured, it will take very little time to keep it sharp. Rarely do I ever use power sharpeners."

Although he would be happy with any sharpening stones, including sandpaper on glass, Ellenwood prefers monocrystalline diamond plates for most sharpening chores. Because many carving tools are very small, it's better to sharpen them on a Norton-style diamond plate with a continuous surface than the DMT-type of plate that has a perforated or interrupted surface, as shown in **Figure 12-10**.

Ellenwood uses a light honing oil on the diamond plates to float the metal particles away. The condition of the edge determines where Ellenwood begins, but he always works through to the finest diamond plate, 1,200-grit, then strops the tool on leather charged with white honing compound in stick form because "It cuts fast and will give your tools a mirror polish."

Figure 12-10. Everett Ellenwood sharpens most carving tools freehand on diamond plates; then, he strops on leather charged with honing compound.

Larry Heinonen, woodworker

A writer and craftsman, Larry Heinonen's work has appeared in several of the major woodworking magazines including *Today's Woodworker,* *Woodworkers Journal,* *Woodshop Business News, Wood Magazine,* and *Woodsmith.* His theory on sharpening is to create a hollow grind and then hone the front lip (see **Figure 12-11**).

Figure 12-11. Woodshop writer Larry Heinonen prefers a hollow grind to a flat one because there's less bevel to hone.

"The sharpest edge is obtained when two perfectly flat, polished planes intersect at the appropriate angle," Heinonen says. "I like about 28 degrees, which I find the best compromise between edge sharpness and longevity. It's always a trade-off. Some people neglect to flatten the back of a chisel (see **Figure 12-12**). Doing so is essential.

"The rig I use is simple. The honing guide is from General, the water stone is King ¹⁰⁰⁰/₈₀₀₀-grit, and the bench hook (see **Figure 12-13**) I made. I have always preferred water stones since discovering they abrade the edge very quickly. They come in a variety of grits and combinations, but, bought for 39 dollars several years ago, this

Figure 12-13. A simple bench hook offers a handy way to set up quickly for grinding and honing with bench stones.

combination stone (see **Figure 12-14**) is literally the only one I use for straight edges. It works quickly and is easy to flatten when needed. For lathe chisels and other curved edges, I use a water slip stone. While you can get various grits, for obvious reasons they are not available in combination grits.

"A properly honed edge is easy to spot. The hollow grind makes the polished edge stand out. The edge (see **Figure 12-15**) is literally sharp as a razor. And the hollow grind allows you to resharpen more quickly because you're removing less material than if you were polishing an entire face. Only the top and bottom edges of the bevel are honed."

Figure 12-14. Larry Heinonen uses a medium/fine and a very fine combination stone to hone flat bench chisels and plane irons.

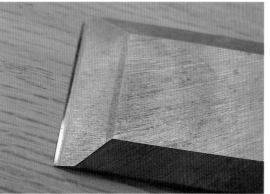

Figure 12-15. A close-up shows Larry Heinonen's hollow grind, which, in the Japanese tradition, leaves only a slim bevel to hone.

Figure 12-12. With the geometry of the bevel in mind, Larry Heinonen uses a very fine water stone to flatten the back of a chisel.

Norm Abram, Woodworker

"The sharpening center I built and use here at the *New Yankee Workshop* is sized to fit in a busy shop and still give me enough space to perform this important task (see **Figure 12-16**). The first decision I made was to make it stationary because even locking casters have some give in them, and that's not a great idea when you're doing precision work. Instead, I went with nylon leveling glides that can be adjusted for an uneven floor.

"The cabinet itself is 34" tall, which is a nice height for most jobs. Sometimes, though, I need to get up to a more comfortable height for some of the sharpening operations, so I built a pull-out step to gain leverage for those tasks. Most of the construction uses ³/₄" birch plywood, and the joinery can be completed with a table saw, router, stacked dado head, and biscuit joiner. The drawers call for some fairly simple sliding dovetails to add strength where it's needed. I also used full

extension slides, so I can see all of the way into the back of each drawer. There's no point in being organized if you can't find things.

"The top is high-density particleboard with a hardwood frame, topped off with high-pressure laminate. I chamfered the edges, and it delivers a nice, clean finish that protects the particleboard from stray moisture. And speaking of moisture, I added a paper towel holder because sharpening can get a little messy at times.

"We do some metalworking here at *New Yankee Workshop* every now and then, so I bolted a 6¹/₂" machinist's vise to the top. Beside that are the other two elements of my system, a desk light and a Tormek slow-rotation, water-cooled grinder. Too much heat draws the temper out of steel, and this machine stops that from happening. It reminds me of the old treadle

Figure 12-16. Norm Abram's sharpening station has a wet/dry grinder, a metalworking vise, and storage space for bench stones.

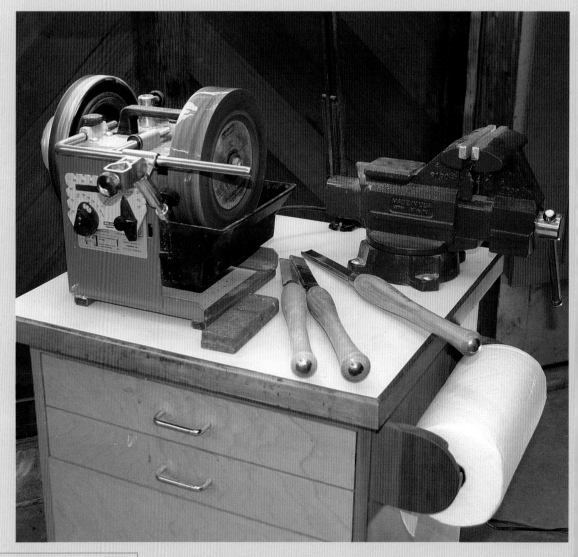

wheels you can still find in antique shops here in New England, except you don't have to turn it by hand. When sharpening, I move the tool from side to side to even up wear on the stone and keep it flat. The machine comes with a gauge that lets me set the bevel quickly (25 degrees for most chisels). The stone is a bit unusual because you change grits by dressing it with a grading stone, which lets you move between grinding and honing without ever shutting down. After honing, a leather stropping wheel on the outside of the machine polishes the bevel and removes the burr in a couple of quick passes. I charge the strop with 6000-grit aluminum oxide compound.

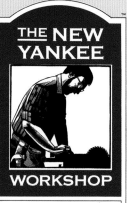

"For me, the ultimate test for an edge is something that sharpening expert Jeff Farris showed me on an episode of the show. If a tool can slice across a sheet of paper like a razor blade, it's sharp enough for wood. Along with the video of the sharpening station episode (item 0011), a measured drawing is available for this project (see **Figure 12-17**), which includes a cutting diagram for the plywood and a materials list. For more information, visit the *New Yankee Workshop* online at *www.newyankee.com*, or call us at (800)-892-0110."

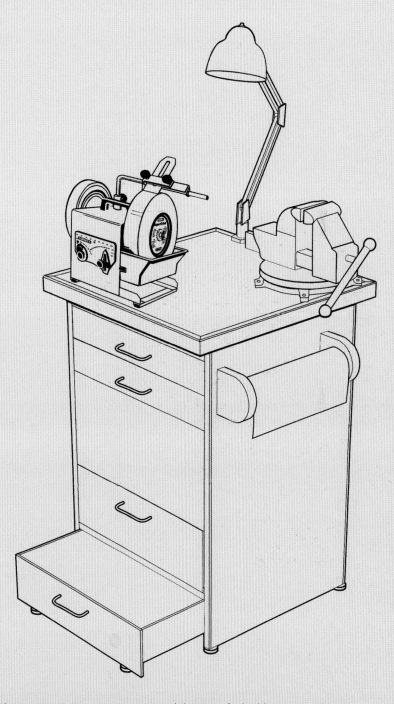

Figure 12-17. You can get measured drawings for building Norm Abram's sharpening station from *www.newyankee.com*.

David J. Marks, furniture maker

Teacher, builder, and two-time Niche Award winner David J. Marks of Santa Rosa, California (see **Figure 12-18**), has been featured on HGTV's *Modern Masters*, and also hosts his own television show, *Wood Works*. The show, on the DIY channel, features step-by-step instructions for building contemporary studio furniture Marks has designed (see **Figure 12-19**).

When he grinds and hones in his own shop (see **Figure 12-20**), Marks uses "a slow-speed grinder (1,725 rpm) to hollow grind my plane blades. For sharpening, I like a combination of water stones. Mounted inside the large thick block of fir in the photograph (see **Figure 12-19**) are a King 800-grit water stone (which is my coarse stone), a King 1,200-grit water stone (medium), and a Norton 8,000-grit water stone as my fine stone.

"I also have some Shapton stones, which I recommend to students if they want to upgrade. For the Shaptons, I am using the 1,000-grit as a coarse stone, the 5,000-grit as medium, and the 8,000-grit as fine. The Shaptons are available all the way to 15,000-grit.

"In the background, you can see a granite slab with some 220-grit wet/dry sandpaper, which I use for flattening the water stones. The Shapton stones are a harder, ceramic stone, so for those I recommend a diamond plate."

Figure 12-19. The exquisite joinery in David J. Marks' dovetail bench is due, in large part, to his devotion to having sharp tools.

Figure 12-20. A complete grinding, lapping (granite slab), and honing setup is shown on the workbench of David J. Marks

Figure 12-18. From small bench to workbench, David J. Marks' attention to detail and his breathtaking artistry leave us spellbound.

Courtesy David J. Marks and Virginia Marks

Figure 12-21. David J. Marks' sharpening session begins with lapping water stones with wet/dry paper on a perfectly flat granite slab.

Ellis Hein, woodturner

In the April 2002 issue of *Woodworker's Journal*, Ellis Hein explained a concept he calls "inside out" turning. He tapes four square blanks together, turns them as one, and then removes the tape. Then he turns each one 180 degrees before gluing them together. The result is the inside of his vessel has been shaped before the outside is ever touched (see **Figure 12-22**). (For more information, visit *www.woodworking. com/article.cfm?article=97*).

Living on the toes of Wyoming's Rockies, Hein is far removed from a ready source of hardwood. He turns every species that is available, including osage orange fence posts, locust, willow, and mountain mahogany. Working in so many scrub species, he comes across some interesting grain patterns. Needless to say, Hein believes in sharp tools.

"Like most turners," he says, "I use a grinder to create the shape I'm looking for on gouges. I prefer an 8" model to lessen the hollow grind, and the machine I use is equipped with a work light and decent spark guards. For stones, I use blue and white friable wheels (see **Figure 12-23**)."

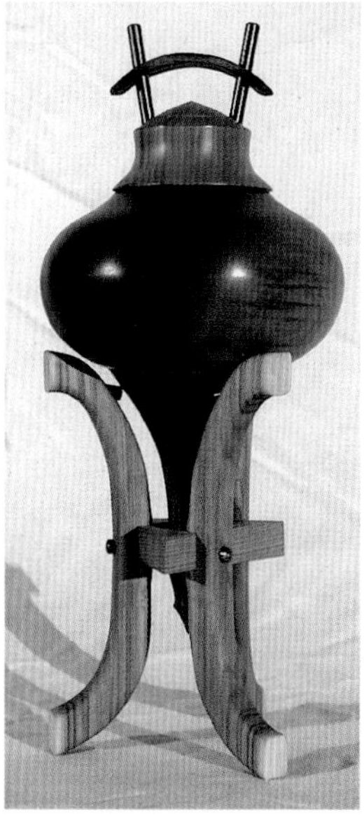

Hein wears reliable dust masks and safety glasses when sharpening. His basement shop is well lit and comfortable, but he has plans for a new shop a little way out of town where he will rely on some "new" old technology: straw bale construction, which is a medieval technique revived in the twentieth century. An innovative thinker

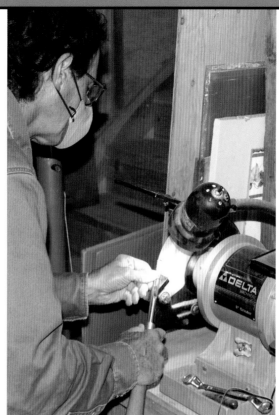

Courtesy Ellis Hein

Courtesy Ellis Hein

Figure 12-23.
Ellis Hein, who developed "inside out" turning, has been grinding gouges so long that he now does it freehand.

Figure 12-24.
Ellis Hein follows up the grinding process with a quick stropping on a paper disk charged with buffing compound.

with a wonderful sense of proportion, his work has been featured in *Woodworker's Journal* and online at *www.woodworking.com*.

"After grinding," Hein explains, "I strop on the drill press (see **Figure 12-24**) using a 6" paper wheel charged with rouge. I've had the wheel for years, and it doesn't seem to be breaking down." An elaborate maze of dust collection hoses works around the drill press and the lathe behind it, emphasizing the importance of clean air in a sharpening environment.

Figure 12-20. Sharp lathe tools are the secret to perfect curves on *Heaven-Sent Bowl* by noted turner Ellis Hein.

David Nittmann, woodturner

Although David Nittman holds a master's degree from Colorado State, he is more at home in a woodshop than in an office. He claims "an obsession" with the lathe and is a member of several turning groups. Nittman does put all that education to some use, however. He is a faculty member of both the Arrowmont School of Arts and Crafts, and the John C. Campbell Folk School in North Carolina.

There's a bit of sharpening history in **Figure 12-25**, Nittman grinding. That small hand-cranked grindstone on the shelf above his electric grinder once belonged to his grandfather. Note the oversized stone on his regular grinder, which is designed to reduce the hollow in grinds. Note, too, the excellent lighting around his sharpening station. Long experience allows him to grind freehand some of the time. The key is knowing how a lathe tool shape should look and being able to imagine it before he turns on the grinder.

"My signature work is the basket illusion," Nitttman says on his website. "Using rare, nonfigured woods, I turn, burn, and dye to create the visual and tactile impression of a woven

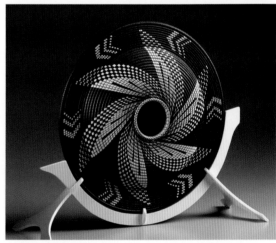

Figure 12-26. Basket illusion turnings by David Nittman.

form. A subset of this work is the bodydrum, a decorative functional instrument. The Corn Mother Series combines the basket illusion and detailed carving."

As if being both a carver and a turner isn't enough, Nittman and partner Cindy Drozda also have a complete cabinet shop in their Rocky Mountain studio. Nittman's work (see **Figure 12-26**) is widely exhibited and has been juried into the best national art/craft shows, including the Smithsonian, the Philadelphia Museum of Art, the American Craft Exposition, and the Washington Craft Show.

Figure 12-25. In high demand as a teacher and demonstrator, David Nittmann sharpens his turning tools freehand on an oversized wheel.

Courtesy David Nittmann

Bill Tarleton, woodturner

One of the busiest woodworkers in America, Bill Tarleton spends a great deal of his time helping other folks. If he's not building furniture for the Concord Veterans' Center, he's making toys for needy children. The wood he turns (see **Figure 12-27**) is "collected mostly from San Francisco East Bay city trees taken down by storms, street or home repairs, or disease. Milling is done with a chainsaw and lots of heavy lifting. Curing is done either by letting the rough-cut wood air dry and then turning it on a lathe, or the green fresh-cut wood is lathe turned into a finished item and then allowed to dry."

Tarleton likes to work with metal, and he makes most of his own sharpening attachments from scrap material. He made a mount for an 8" slow grinder on the tailstock end of his lathe. The lathe grinder station "is easily removed by loosening a single bolt, should it be in the way. It is extremely handy when turning several bowls, one after another. I seldom use the tailstock when turning a bowl. I do use it, however, when using a bowl saver," a device for removing the core of a bowl intact so another, smaller bowl may be turned from it.

Tarleton continues, "In the lathe grinder station (see **Figure 12-28**), you can see my homemade tool sharpening jigs at each wheel. The left wheel has the adjustable pivot bar for a Wolverine fingernail gouge jig. The right-hand wheel has a short piece of angle iron used to lay a bowl gouge in, and rotate the gouge for sharpening. The magnetic protractor is set on a second grinder (see **Figure 12-29**) to establish the bevel angle for various scrapers. It is a very useful tool for setting almost any angle on the grinder."

Figure 12-27. A segmented vessel, created by Bill Tarleton, has been in the author's private collection for a few years.

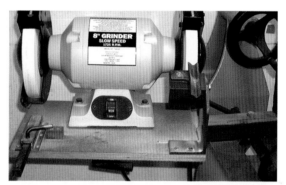

Courtesy Bill Tarleton

Figure 12-28. The grinder attached to the tailstock of Bill Tarleton's lathe saves time, and it can be removed by releasing one bolt.

Courtesy Bill Tarleton

Figure 12-29. Bill Tarleton says this welder's device, a plastic angle gauge with a magnetic base, is ideal for setting tool rest angles.

Kevin Neelley, woodturner

Kevin Neelley, like so many elite woodworkers, is a generous soul who gives a lot back to his craft. On his Website, he provides what is essentially a free tutorial on segmented turning. One of the pages "is intended for the beginning segmented bowl maker," he says. "This is basically a no-math approach to segmented bowl design. I have made three design sheets that will help the beginner through the design phase. Using these sheets, I have designed a nine-layered bowl using twelve-sided frame-mitered rings. The Webpage will walk you through the design steps." One of Neelley's segmented vessels is shown in **Figure 12-30**.

"My grinder," he continues, "is a Baldor, running at 1,800 rpm (see **Figure 12-31**). I use a Oneway Wolverine jig for sharpening all of my lathe tools, except the skews. Those I grind on the other wheel (see **Figure 12-32**), using the tool rest. This seems to work better, especially for oval skews. I don't use a strop, slip stone, or diamond file, just a quick zing on the grinder."

Figure 12-30. Segmented vessel turned by Kevin Neelley.

Figure 12-31. Kevin Neelley favors a slow grinder (1,800 rpm) with a Wolverine jig for shaping the profiles of his turning tools.

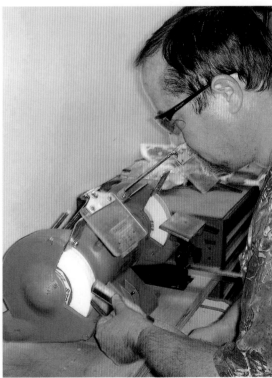

Figure 12-32. Kevin Neelley sharpens flat and oval skews on the tool rest of the grinder, using friable wheels and no jig.

Courtesy Kevin Neelley

Raymond Lanham, woodturner

A master turner who specializes in segmented vessels and platters, such as the example shown in **Figure 12-33**, Raymond Lanham of Dallas, Texas, has spent a great deal of time teaching "from the Midwest and the Southwest, to West and Central Africa, and even the scorched Outback in Australia. I have been blessed to work with a vast array of exotic wood species. As a result, I have sought to combine and experiment with these rare and beautiful woods."

Lanham says he differentiates "sharpening (refining the cutting edge) from grinding (shaping the cutting edge). My sharpening system is bolted to the end of my bowl lathe, which isn't an original idea. In fact, I borrowed the concept from Herman De Vries, a woodturner from Winnipeg, Canada, who also told me about the blue zirconia belt, which I purchased from Lee Valley Tools. The belt is used to grind stainless steel and has no trouble putting a very nice edge on high-speed steel turning tools. I've mounted it on the end of my lathe (see **Figure 12-34**) so when a tool starts to dull, it's very easy to take one step left, turn on the belt sander, revive the edge of my scraper, and then move one step back . . . and never miss a beat. It's easy to keep the tools sharp when I don't have to do much to get to my sharpening station."

Courtesy Raymond Lanham

Figure 12-33. Raymond Lanham's *Star of Texas* bowl won a blue ribbon at the Texas State Fair.

Courtesy Raymond Lanham

Figure 12-34. Raymond Lanham bolted a 1" belt sander directly to the end of his bowl lathe, and he runs zirconia belts for sharpening.

Figure 12-35. A doctoral candidate and father of three, Darrell Feltmate finds great satisfaction in the reclusive tranquility of his woodturning shop.

Darrell Feltmate, woodturner

A Nova Scotian with two kids in graduate school and a third who is volunteering in Thailand, Darrell Feltmate (see **Figure 12-35**) needed something to take his mind off things on those cold winter nights. So, he did what any stressed parent would do. He went back to college and entered a Doctor of Ministry (DMin) degree program. An example of Feltmate's work is shown in **Figure 12-36**.

"One of my peculiarities," Feltmate says, "is the enjoyment I get from making many of my own tools and jigs." Once they are made, he likes to share the results with beginning turners. For example, he wanted a set of Cole jaws for reverse turning bowl bottoms, but couldn't justify the price. So, he made a set of bottoming jaws (see **Figure 12-37**), with which he is very pleased. For details and an illustrated step-by-step account of the process, turners are invited to visit his Website, *www.aroundthewoods.com*.

Another jig shown in great detail on his Website is the collection of wooden blocks stored around his grinder. They are part of a shop-built system he uses for sharpening gouges. The blocks have different-length dowels extending from their bottom faces, which rest

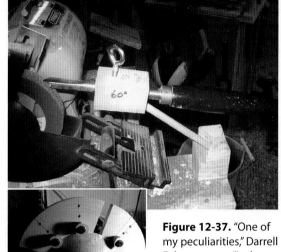

Figure 12-37. "One of my peculiarities," Darrell Feltmate says, "is the enjoyment I get from making many of my own tools and jigs."

in a pocket that slides in and out from under the left side of the grinder, shown in **Figure 12-38**. By combining a certain-length dowel with a given amount of extension, Feltmate can dial up any angle he wants on his bevels.

"For the beginning turner, and unfortunately for many long-timers, sharpening is a mystery," Feltmate says. "Sharp tools make for great shavings, better surfaces off the tool, less sanding, and more fun. Turning with a dull tool is hard work and leaves a lot of work, with lots and lots of sanding."

Figure 12-36. Natural-edge bowl by Darrell Feltmate.

He continued, "The left wheel on my grinder has been replaced with a wheel that turns it into a sharpener. It's aluminum oxide, and white is supposed to be the best for woodturners since we use high-speed steel in our tools. White cuts the high-speed steel well and runs cool. Actually, the color of the wheel has little, if anything, to do with aluminum oxide. It is a coloring system that lets the manufacturer see in a glance what bonding agent has been used in making the wheel. White wheels have a very friable, or easily wearing, binding agent. This allows the aluminum oxide to wear quickly, which gives a cooler, cleaner wheel, but it also does wear quickly. That means the wheel may need to be dressed more often for wear, but less for dirt. Regardless, I find the white wheels wear too fast for me. What I am using now for general sharpening is a brown aluminum oxide wheel, 80-grit. The 60-grit will work, and 100-grit works with jigs, but I believe 80-grit gives me the best compromise between fast sharpening and a great edge."

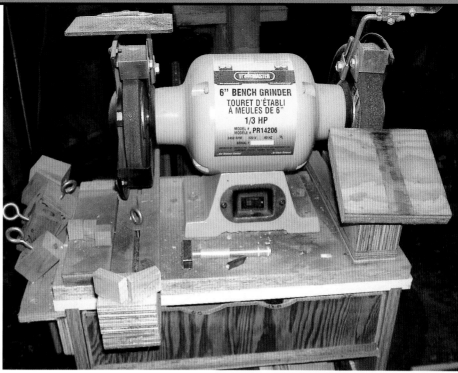

Courtesy Darrell Feltmate

Figure 12-38. Darrell Feltmate shares all the construction details of this shop-built gouge-sharpening jig on his website.

David Reed Smith, woodturner

In any shop tour, it would be a shame not to include the innovative and highly imaginative sharpening stations of wood artist David Reed Smith (see **Figure 12-39**). Most of the projects Smith tackles are small, so he spends a lot of time sharpening small tools and cutters. The ingenious and seemingly complex sharpening station shown here is actually quite simple.

"The system is based upon a cheap 8" drill press," he says. "The drill head is mounted upside down. The platform is mounted above it and supports the rest of the system. The drill press is used to drive a quick-change set of abrasive disks. Lubricant cooling is provided for all but touchup sharpening. Accuracy is ensured by using the same jig for everything, from the roughest grind to the finest hone. Three different jig supports are included. A multiple-angle platform sharpens roughing gouges (and also works nicely on chisels and plane irons), skews, and scrapers. A V-block analog sharpens detail spindles and bowl gouges. And a straight-line reference sharpens a variety of other tools." Smith's plans for his station are completely free and are available as a download from his Website (*www.davidreedsmith.com*).

Figure 12-39. Looking like a piece of modern sculpture, David Reed Smith's ingenious sharpening station gets the job done.

Mark Koons, furniture maker

Award-winning artist, builder, photographer, writer, and curator Mark Koons (see **Figure 12-40**) is a sensible guy. He placed his sharpening station in front of a large window to take advantage of natural daylight. He used the same concept when building his shop—the upper floor on the south side is a solar dry kiln. A pioneer in an ancient technique, Koons has spent several years perfecting the art of bent micro-lamination. His *Simple Chair* (see **Figure 12-41**) is a poem in wood, elegantly twisting and turning to receive and welcome the occupant.

That awareness of ergonomics also led Koons to set his sharpening equipment a little higher off the floor than most people so he doesn't have to bend while honing. Taking the daylight concept a bit further, he equipped his station with a work light and a magnifying light (see **Figure 12-42**), again underscoring that maxim that good light makes good work. Koons favors water stones and keeps them in a plastic salad crisper drawer from an old refrigerator, which acts as a pond.

"Unfortunately," he says, "I have to take them in the house in winter to prevent them from freezing and cracking. I use a piece of ¼" mirror as a lapping plate, covering it with wet/dry paper, and one of the most important parts of my sharpening setup is a simple spray bottle for water. I have gathered enough honing guides over the decades to sharpen any blade, any width, at any angle."

Courtesy Mark Koons

Figure 12-40. Furniture artist Mark Koons of Wheatland, Wyoming likes to build his own grinders so he can slow them down to 1,000 rpm or less.

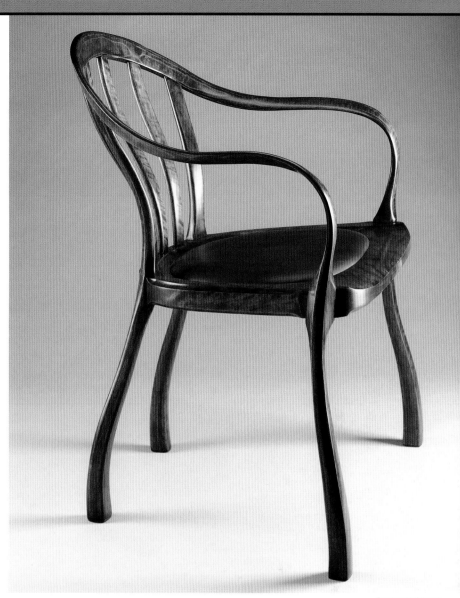

Courtesy Mark Koons

Figure 12-41. A former student of Sam Maloof, Mark Koons devoted hundreds of hours to the design of his *Simple Chair*.

Courtesy Mark Koons

Figure 12-42. Furniture artist Mark Koons takes full advantage of the natural daylight washing over his sharpening station.

John English, woodworker

My sharpening station (see **Figures 12-43** and **12-44**) was built as a project for *Woodcraft Magazine*. It's a frame-and-panel mahogany cabinet with a couple of drawers, a raised-panel door, and a shop-built bench grinder. The grinder runs at 1,150 rpm and 1,725 rpm, and it uses an 8" friable white stone. In addition to the grinder, I use a slow wet stone, a 1" x 30" belt sander, a desk lamp, and a large machinist's vise. The grinder tool rest is very sturdy and has a miter gauge slot so that I can grind at 90 degrees to the long edges of a tool. The ball bearing arbor also holds an 8" firm-stitched buffing pad, which I like to charge with Flexcut's Gold Compound. A shelf in the station holds a white plastic basin with some glass gemstones that hold the water stones up off the bottom, avoiding dry spots. On the top, a couple of L-shaped brackets hold a plate-glass lapping plate. Releasing two large knobs allows the entire grindstone housing to be removed for maintenance. Inside the compartment behind the panel door is a three-drawer plastic office organizer, which holds all of my various stones (diamond, oil, and water). Complete plans for this sharpening station (and its built-in grinder) begin on page 151.

Figure 12-43. Author John English displays his sharpening station. Plans for this station begin on page 151.

Figure 12-44. The back view of John English's sharpening station shows the shop-built bench grinder.

Sam Maloof, furniture maker

Perhaps the most naturally gifted teacher in woodworking, furniture maker Sam Maloof of Alto Loma, California, has an easygoing, conversational tone that immediately relaxes an audience. His modest nature, in light of his vast talent, is refreshing and inspiring. Instantly likeable, he enjoys people and is genuinely interested in their lives and work.

Maloof and his wife, Beverley, are generous to a fault. Among their philanthropic endeavors are being major contributors to the Anderson Ranch Arts Center in Colorado, and the Sam and Alfreda Maloof Foundation for Arts and Crafts. The latter "recognizes and celebrates fine artists and craftsmen who skillfully create timeless treasures with their hands." The foundation is the legacy of Sam and his late wife and partner of 50 years, Alfreda. Its mission is "to perpetuate excellence in craftsmanship, encourage artists, and make available to the public the treasure house that the Maloofs lovingly created." For more information, visit *www.malooffoundation.org.*

"My sharpening stones," Maloof says, "are made by David Powell in Wellesley, Massachusetts. I use them for plane irons, and also to sharpen chisels."

The stones he is referring to are a fairly new product line from Powell Manufacturing. They have been around long enough to prove their value. What Maloof really likes is they put a very slight curl or arc across a bevel so a plane working a board wider than its own iron doesn't leave trails across the surface. The patent for the stones is held by David Powell (the co-founder of DMT) and Professor Toshio Odate of the Pratt Institute, a noted sculptor and woodworker in the Japanese tradition.

The stones are actually not stone at all. They begin with a cast-iron plate that is given a concave, cylindrical surface with a very large radius (slight curve). The surface is then coated with monocrystalline diamond, by electroplating nickel. There are about two million diamonds

Figure 12-45. Sam Maloof uses diamond-coated plates developed by Toshio Odate that leave a very slight radius on a tool's bevel.

on each 3" x 7" plate. Looking at the stones on Maloof's simple bench (see **Figure 12-45**), the black ones are extra coarse (220 grit/60 micron); blue are coarse (325 grit/45 micron); red are fine (600 grit/25 micron); and the green ones are extra fine (1200 grit/9 micron). There's an extra stone at the left of the bench, and that's a convex version with the same curve to it. It is used to dress some very fine- and polishing-grit water stones, lapping them so that the tops of the stones actually become mildly concave. Maloof can use the water stones to hone and polish to a mirror finish, without losing the shape he has gained by grinding with the diamond stones. He switches to 4,000-grit and 8,000-grit to do that.

We began this journey with Sam Maloof, and it's only fitting we should end with a look at how he sharpens. No other figure has influenced woodworking in the past 60 years to the extent he has. Through his teaching and writing (see **Figure 12-44**) and the unprecedented access he has given to journalists, he has reached an astounding number of woodworkers and changed the way they work, design, and respect the medium. His gentle ways and easy speech, his love of life and craft, and his innate integrity are an inspiration and a roadmap for the rest of us.

Thanks, Sam.

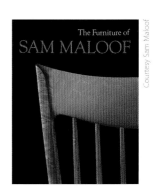

Figure 12-44. Sam Maloof's furniture is celebrated in his book.

Appendix 1

Glossary

Some of these definitions have a different, specific meaning in sharpening than they might have in general use.

Abrasive: A material that uses friction to reduce a softer surface.

Alumina: See aluminum oxide.

Aluminum oxide: A chemical compound of aluminum and oxygen (Al_2O_3), formed under intense heat.

Angle: Where two faces meet.

Angle, included: The sum of the bevel on a cutter and the angle at which it addresses the work.

Arkansas stone: A naturally occurring whetstone found in the Ouachita Mountains of Arkansas.

Back: The flat face of a cutter, usually without a bevel.

Back bevel: A very small bevel added to the back of a cutter, where the primary bevel is on the front.

Bench plane: Any of several tools that hold an iron (blade) at a specified angle to the work.

Bevel: An angle ground on a cutting edge. Many edges have two bevels, a large primary and a small secondary.

Buff: A polishing process that follows grinding and honing to remove scratches, usually done on a wheel.

Burnish: Rolling a burr along the edge of a scraper that has been ground to a 90-degree angle so it will shave wood.

Burr: A thin, rough ridge on the edge of a piece of metal.

Camber: An almost indiscernible arc along the cutting edge, designed to eliminate ridges at the edge of the cutter.

Carbide: A compound of carbon, usually containing tungsten or titanium, which results in very hard, brittle metal.

Carbon steel: Alloy of iron and carbon with almost no other elements present. The higher the carbon content, the harder the alloy is.

Carborundum: Name trademarked by Edward Goodrich Acheson in the 1890s for the compound silicon carbide (SiC).

Ceramics: Inorganic agents (not metals), which are formed by heat and can be extremely hard and abrasive.

Chip breaker: A steel plate with a slight curve that rests on a blade (plane iron) and rolls a shaving up and away.

Chromium oxide: A green brick of honing compound (Cr_2O_3) that may cause respiratory problems for some people.

Cryogenics: An industrial process using extremely low temperatures to treat steel so it will hold a better edge.

Crystolon: A fast-cutting man-made stone from Norton, a subsidiary of Saint-Gobain Abrasives Inc.

Deburring: Removing the ridge of metal created behind a bevel during grinding or honing, by stropping or buffing.

Diamond: Man-made or natural industrial diamond crystals (not gem quality) and powders, used as abrasives.

Diamond paste: Paste of diamond dust in several micron grades, used with special fluid to produce a mirror finish.

Dressing wheel: Grindstone edges are cleaned and squared up with a dressing wheel when glazed, clogged, or distorted.

Dull: A tool which tears wood fibers rather than slicing through them effortlessly.

File: A hard, brittle steel tool that used to be a viable option for sharpening, and still has some limited uses.

Grind: A subjective term that usually refers only to the creation of a primary bevel on a cutter. (See also hone.)

Hardness: Describing that property in steel, harder cuts quicker but is more brittle and subject to fragmenting.

Helix: A term used to describe the twist on twist drills.

Hollow grind: The very slight arc created when a tool is ground on the curved edge of a wheel rather than on the flat side.

Hone: A finer process than grinding, honing most often refers to the production of a polished secondary bevel.

India stone: Norton's term for a line of man-made oilstones.

Iron (plane): See plane iron.

Japanese chisel: These have a soft, thick layer of iron laminated to a hard layer of steel that actually holds the edge.

Japanese plane: Pulled rather than pushed, their blades have a hollow back that reduces the work of sharpening.

Japanese water stone: Traditionally quarried in the Narutaki District near Kyoto, but now are mostly man-made composites.

Jig: In sharpening, anything which holds the blade at the correct angle to the stone, and is repeatable.

Kell, Richard: A British inventor who makes some of the world's highest-quality honing guides and jigs.

Knife: The blades in a jointer or planer are known in woodworking as knives.

Lapping plate: Flat granite, plate glass, or metal to which wet/dry sandpaper is attached to flatten the soles of planes.

Leather strop: A strap or a motorized wheel of leather, charged with honing compound and used to polish an edge.

Lubricant: Oil and water are primarily cleaners, not lubricants, in the world of sharpening.

Molybdenum: An element (Mo) with an extremely high melting point (4753°F), used in tool steel to add heat resistance.

Nagura stone: Used to create swarf on very fine Japanese water stones that are too hard to create their own.

Novaculite: A chert (quartz), quarried in the Ouachita (Washita) Mountains (Arkansas and Oklahoma), used as a whetstone.

Oilstone: A natural or man-made stone that uses oil or kerosene as a cleaner.

Ouachita: See Washita oilstone and novaculite.

Plane iron: The common term for the blade in a bench plane.

Polishing: Removing scratches to deliver a mirrorlike finish that can be attained through buffing or stropping.

Primary bevel: The larger bevel on a chisel or plane iron, usually achieved by grinding. (See also secondary bevel.)

Rake: The angle at which the front face of a saw tooth meets the work. (See also saw set.)

Relief: An area removed behind a cutter to prevent any other part of the blade or tool from contacting the work.

Rockwell scale: A measure of hardness produced by hitting a piece of steel and precisely measuring the indent.

Saw set: The angle(s) at which the teeth of a saw lean to either side.

Secondary bevel: A small, second bevel created along the cutting edge by honing with fine bench stones.

Sharp: Steel with an acutely angled edge capable of slicing through wood fibers rather than tearing them.

Side grind: On turning gouges, creating a fingernail profile requires some grinding up along the sides of the tool.

Silicon carbide: See carborundum.

Skew: A tool used in turning and carving that has a compound angle on the business end.

Slip stone: Shaped stones (oil, water, or diamond) that can reach into curved, round, or small areas of cutters.

Spring steel: Steel with medium to high carbon content that has a "memory" of its original form and reverts to it.

Star dressing wheel: A steel wheel of star-shaped plates used to dress grindstones, now being replaced by diamond dressers.

Steel: An alloy of iron and carbon that may also include nickel, manganese, chromium, vanadium, or tungsten.

Stone: In sharpening, a natural or man-made abrasive in wheel, block, or slip shape, used to sharpen steel edges.

Strop: See leather strop.

Swarf: The lubricating debris of sharpening includes either oil or water and fine metal filings and stone grit.

Tungsten: The chemical element W, it has an extremely high-melting point and makes steel both hard and brittle.

Vanadium: The chemical element V increases the hardness of steel and reduces the effects of metal fatigue.

Washita oilstone: See novaculite.

Water stone: Any stone, natural or man-made, which uses water as a cleaning agent.

Wet/dry paper: Usually black, with silicon carbide abrasive bonded to paper or cloth with a waterproof resin.

Wet grind: A slowly revolving stone that uses a constant source of water to cool the steel.

Wheels: On bench grinders, they should be soft, friable aluminum oxide, and the hardness should be in the J to K range.

Whetstone: Traditionally, an oilstone.

Appendix 2

Supplier Websites

Carbide Processors, Inc.
www.carbideprocessors.com/Brazing/book

Christopher Biggs honing jig
http://members.optushome.com.au/cjbiggs/
shed/sharpening-jig/index.html

David Ellsworth turning tool jig
www.ellsworthstudios.com

David Reed Smith sharpening station
www.davidreedsmith.com

Delta grinders
www.deltamachinery.com

DMT diamond and ceramic stones
www.DMTsharp.com

Drill Doctor sharpeners
www.drilldoctor.com

Garrett Wade woodworking tools
www.garrettwade.com

Grizzly wet/dry grinders
www.grizzlyimports.com

GRS Power Hone
www.grstools.com

Hartville Tools, diamond paste
www.hartvilletool.com

HDC sharpeners
www.homier.com

**Japan Woodworker, Japanese tools
and water stones**
www.japanwoodworker.com

JET machinery
www.jettools.com

JoolTool sharpener
www.jooltool.com

Kell honing guides
www.richardkell.co.uk

Lap-Sharp sharpening machine
www.woodartistry.com

Lee Valley Tools
www.leevalley.com

Makita sharpener
www.makita.com

M.POWER sharpeners
www.m-powertools.com

Norm Abram sharpening station plans
www.newyankee.com

**Norton grinding wheels, sharpening stones,
and diamond plates**
www.nortonconsumer.com

Oneway Manufacturing
www.oneway.on.ca

Plasplugs sharpeners
www.plasplugsusa.com

Powell Manufacturing, Odate sharpening plates
www.planeperfect.com

Ridgid machinery
www.ridgid.com

Rockler Woodworking and Hardware
www.rockler.com

Scheppach sharpening machine
www.scheppach.com

Sharpenset sharpening system
www.sharpenset.co.uk

Shapton ceramic stones
www.shaptonstones.com

Sherwood/Timbecon
www.timbecon.com.au

Sorby turning tools jig
www.robert-sorby.co.uk

Tormek sharpening systems
www.tormek.us

Veritas Tools
www.veritastools.com

Vintage saws
www.vintagesaws.com

WheelEzze dresser
www.milescraft.com

Woodcraft Supply
www.woodcraft.com

Woodcut Tools, Tru-Grind jig
www.shop.woodcut-tools.com

Woodsmith cabinet scraper clamp
www.woodsmithstore.com

Woodtek sharpening machine
http://woodworker.com

Woodworker's Supply
http://woodworker.com

Appendix 3

John English Sharpening Center

This handy station houses all your tools and supplies

Many woodworkers store sharpening supplies here and there throughout the shop, out of sight and out of mind. Having an organized station focuses attention on this essential task, transforming a chore into a satisfying experience. My station has a 1" belt sander, a horizontal wet stone grinder, a work light (essential!), a lapping plate, an 8" vertical grinder, and an 8" two-wheel grinder. The station is not mobile, because even the best locking casters allow a little play—not what you want in a sharpening station.

You can choose whether to purchase a slow-speed 8" commercial grinder or to build the motor-and-mandrel version shown in the drawings. Either way, the cabinet construction is almost the same.

The cabinet consists of four simple frames, glued and screwed together. The frames are built with butt and tongue-and-groove joints. With a low budget, I chose inexpensive ¼" lauan plywood for the sides and mahogany for the frames. The back of the cabinet is a slightly more complex version of the sides, with four stiles and three rails. Note that a small opening at the top left of the cabinet back provides access to the grinder motor. If you choose a factory-built grinder, you could eliminate this opening, but I would recommend leaving it in place as a storage cubby.

The rest of the cabinet innards are contained in a single H-shaped subassembly that drops into place. It is a simple plywood construction, with two pairs of hardwood drawer slides inset in grooves, as shown in the drawing. The subassembly is 29" tall—½" shorter than the cabinet sides—to leave room for the cleats that will support the top. Because I planned to store my water stone basin inside the cabinet, I used melamine-coated chipboard for the shelf.

The worktop is solid-surface material, such as Corian, which is non-porous and very flat. Choose a light color to reflect light and improve visibility. Instead of making a single shelf for the compartment behind the door, consider investing about $20 in plastic containers that stack together to create a completely dust-free environment. For my water stones, I purchased a plastic basin and lined the bottom with inexpensive glass beads. The beads suspend the stones so water can soak in equally from all sides.

Every sharpening station needs a perfectly flat lapping plate for truing the soles of planes and the backs of plane irons. This one began with a piece of ¼"-thick plate glass purchased at a local glass shop, where they polished the edges to remove any sharp corners. It is sized to take one and a half sheets of wet/dry emery paper on each face, 150- and 180-grit, applied with spray adhesive.

Mount a friable 8" white aluminum oxide 60-grit stone on one side of the grinder and an 8" x 1" stitched buffing wheel or leather stropping wheel on the other. The white wheel is softer than a standard silicon carbide gray wheel. It breaks down more easily and presents new facets to the tool more readily, making it the ideal stone for fine tool steel.

The tool rest and buffing plate shown in the drawings are sized to fit my shop-made grinder, so you will need to fiddle with the dimensions to make these parts work with a commercial grinder. The tool rest needs to be flexible enough to present tools to the wheel at a variety of angles, and yet be stable and solid. With that in mind, the top of the rest is a full 6" wide.

After installing everything, sand all of the parts and apply the finish of your choice. With a couple of coats of clear poly on my mahogany center, it looks as sharp as the edges it creates on tools.

Appendix 3 *(continued)*

John English Sharpening Center

Hardware

17" continuous piano hinge & screws*, #27H48, woodcraft.com
¼" x 1½" hex head bolts (4)
¼" nylon locking nuts (4)
¼" fender washers (8)
3" lag screws (4)
1" L-plates brackets (4)
⁵⁄₁₆"-18 knobs (2), #142906, woodcraft.com
⁵⁄₁₆"-18 threaded inserts (2), Ace Hardware (used in article)
⁵⁄₁₆"-18 threaded inserts (2), #12K60, woodcraft.com (alternate)
Cabinet pull, Amerock #BP19010-SS or similar
1½" socket head cap screw, (2), match thread to pull
¼" OD x ½" long spacers (2)
³⁄₁₆" ID fender washers (2)
¼"-20 x 1½" stud knobs (5), #142230, woodcraft.com
¼"-20 threaded inserts (5), #12K50, woodcraft.com
1½" x 5", continuous piano hinges & screws (2)
⁵⁄₁₆" ID washers (2)
Face mount inset hinges (4), #130141, woodcraft.com
Drawer knobs (3), #130147, woodcraft.com
½" #6 roundhead screws (6)
¾" #6 flathead screws (25)
1⅛" drywall screws (45)
1¼" #8 flathead screws (20)
1⅝" #8 flathead screws (60)
2" #8 flathead screws (30)
³⁄₈" walnut plugs (25)
1½" brads (12)
4d finish nails (12)

Components

Motor, ¾-hp, 3450 rpm*
Mandrel, ball bearing, double-threaded*, #04R23, woodcraft.com
6" pulley, for an A belt*
4" pulley, for an A belt*
2" pulleys (2), for an A belt*
V-belt, A40 (length variable)*
Switch, single pole*
Switch plate, standard*
Plastic stacking bins, Sterilite #1804, Wal-Mart
8", white alum. oxide grindstone, 60-grit, #01W48, woodcraft.com
8" x 1" stitched buffing wheel, #07M04, woodcraft.com
Glass beads
Power strip
¼" glass plate

Materials

Water-based clear polyurethane
Sandpaper
Wood glue

* indicates optional parts not needed with a commercial grinder

Cut List

#							
1	Front & back outer stiles (4)	¾"	x	1¼"	x	34½"
2	Front center stile	¾"	x	1½"	x	28"
3	Front top & bottom rails (2)	¾"	x	1½"	x	35"
4	Front drawer rails (2)	¾"	x	1½"	x	20¼"
5	Side stiles (4)	¾"	x	2"	x	34½"
6	Side rails (4)	¾"	x	1½"	x	23⅝"
7	Side panels (2)	¼"	x	23⅝"	x	28⅝"
8	Back top & bottom rails (2)	¾"	x	1½"	x	35⅝"
9	Back center stiles (2)	¾"	x	1½"	x	28⅝"
10	Back center rail	¾"	x	1½"	x	13⅞"
11	Left back panel	¼"	x	13⅞"	x	17⅛"
12	Middle back panel	¼"	x	6⅛"	x	28⅝"
13	Right back panel	¼"	x	13⅞"	x	28⅝"
14	Long bottom cleats (2)	¾"	x	1"	x	37½"
15	Short bottom cleats (2)	¾"	x	1"	x	25½"
16	Bottom	¾"	x	25½"	x	37½"
17	H sides (2)	¾"	x	25¼"	x	29"
18	H shelf	¾"	x	21"	x	13"
19	H back	¾"	x	21"	x	11¾"
20	H spacers (2)	¼"	x	¾"	x	29"
21	Motor mounting plate*	¾"	x	11"	x	17"
22	Cleats (3), trim to fit	¾"	x	2½"		
23	Drawer slides, trim to fit (4)	¾"	x	¾"	x	25¼"
24	Drawer fronts & backs (4)	¾"	x	6¾"	x	19¼"
25	Drawer sides (4)	¾"	x	6¾"	x	23¾"
26	Drawer bottoms (2)	½"	x	19⅜"	x	17½"
27	Drawer faces (2)	¾"	x	8"	x	20¾"
28	Front door stiles (2)	¾"	x	2½"	x	28½"
29	Front door rails (2)	¾"	x	2½"	x	9¼"
30	Front door panel, plywood	¼"	x	9¼"	x	24⅜"
31	Back door stiles (2), version 1	¾"	x	2½"	x	10½"
32	Back door rails (2), version 1	¾"	x	2½"	x	9⅜"
33	Back door panel, plywood, ver. 1	¼"	x	7¼"	x	10½"
34	Back door, solid, version 2	¾"	x	9⅜"	x	13¾"
35	Tabletop, solid surface	½"	x	30"	x	42"
36	Furring strip	¾"	x	3½"	x	16'
37	Cove molding	¾"	x	¾"	x	14'
38	Mandrel mounting blocks (2)*	2"	x	7"	x	9¾"
39	Mounting block trim*	½"	x	2"	x	72"
40	Switch mounting plate*	½"	x	5⅝"	x	8"
41	Housing back	¾"	x	15¼"	x	14¼"
42	Housing sides (2)	¾"	x	10"	x	14¼"
43	Housing front trim (2)	¼"	x	¾"	x	14¼"
44	Housing top	¾"	x	10¼"	x	15¼"
45	Housing top molding	¾"	x	2"	x	42"
46	Eye guard, clear plastic	⅛"	x	4"	x	14"
47	Eye guard cleat	¾"	x	1¾"	x	15¼"
48	Tool rest base, back	¾"	x	4½"	x	15⅜"
49	Tool rest base, bottom	¾"	x	4"	x	15⅜"
50	Buffing plate	¾"	x	3"	x	6½"
51	Buffing plate support	¾"	x	1¾"	x	3¼"
52	Spark shield, plate brass	¹⁄₁₆"	x	4½"	x	6"
53	Tool rest liners (3), steel	⅛"	x	1"	x	6"
54	Tool rest sub-base	¾"	x	2¾"	x	5"
55	Tool rest sub-base flange (2)	¾"	x	1¾"	x	5"
56	H-frame center	¾"	x	5"	x	3½"
57	H-frame sides (2)	⅜"	x	¾"	x	5¾"
58	H-frame mounting block	¾"	x	5"	x	3"
59	Long stabilizer	¼"	x	¾"	x	9¾"
60	Short stabilizer	¼"	x	¾"	x	7¼"

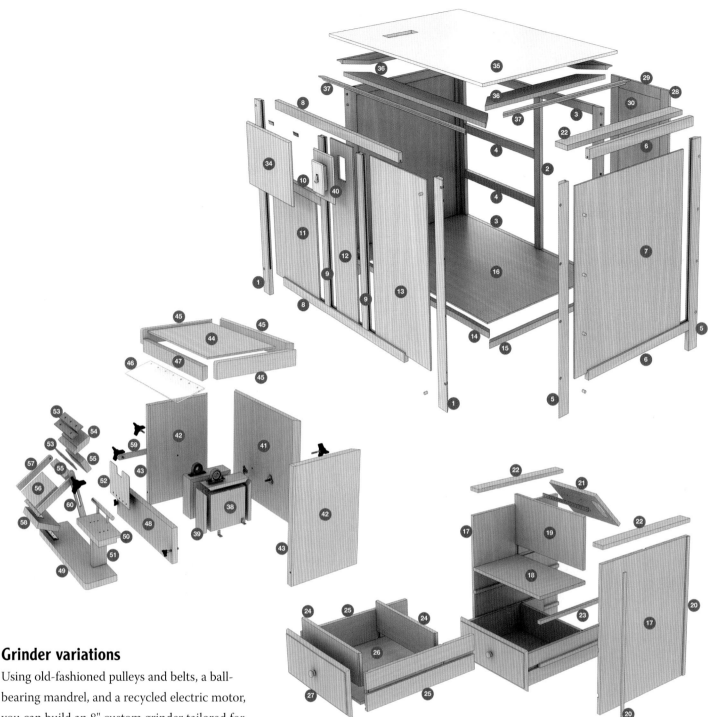

Grinder variations

Using old-fashioned pulleys and belts, a ball-bearing mandrel, and a recycled electric motor, you can build an 8" custom grinder tailored for woodworkers. My version has two speeds, 1,150 rpm and 1,725 rpm. The slower speed works well for both buffing and grinding. At that speed, contact with the 60-grit stone of friable white aluminum oxide generates very little heat. A ¾-hp used capacitor-start motor is ideal (although a ½-hp will work); appliance repair shops are a great source.

If you choose a commercial grinder, I recommend an 8" slow-speed version, not the common 6" high-speed machine. The larger stone delivers a smaller hollow grind (a flatter arc), but the slow speed is its real advantage. You won't need to purchase the motor, mandrel, pulleys, v-belts, the 17-inch piano hinge, or the electrical switch and plate. You also can do without the motor mounting plate (part 21), the mandrel mounting blocks (parts 38 and 39), and the switch plate (part 40). Be sure you make the shelf (part 18) the full depth of the cabinet, and don't omit the storage-space divider (part 19).

Appendix 4

Index

More Great Books from Fox Chapel Publishing

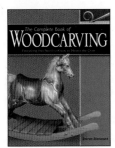

The Complete Book of Woodcarving
By Everett Ellenwood
Comprehensive reference covers every classic style, along with power carving. Also contains 9 projects and helpful resource section.
$24.95
ISBN 978-1-56523-292-1

Foolproof Wood Finishing
By Teri Masaschi
Take the mystery out of finishing with easy-to-follow exercises designed by one of the nation's premier finishing instructors.
$19.95
ISBN 978-1-56523-303-4

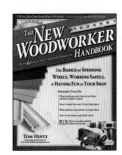

The New Woodworker Handbook
By Tom Hintz
Includes tips, techniq tool overviews, shop setup, and detailed woodworking plans.
$19.95
ISBN 978-1-56523-297-

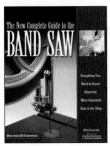

The New Complete Guide to the Band Saw
By Mark Duginske
Learn to master the workshop's most important saw. Contains over 500 photographs and illustrations.
$19.95
ISBN 978-1-56523-318-8

Woodworker's Pocket Reference
By Charlie Self
Everything a woodworker needs to know in an easy-to-read, quick-to-find format.
$14.95
ISBN 978-1-56523-239-6

Learn to Turn
By Barry Gross
An easy-to-follow introduction to woodturning. 8 step step projects includi pepper mill, orname bowls, and more.
$16.95
ISBN 978-1-56523-27

LOOK FOR THESE BOOKS AT YOUR LOCAL BOOKSTORE OR WOODWORKING RETAILER

To order direct, call 800-457-9112 or visit www.FoxChapelPublishing.com

By mail, please send check or money order + $4.00 per book for S&H to:
Fox Chapel Publishing, 1970 Broad Street, East Petersburg, PA 17520

Learn from the Experts

You already know that Fox Chapel Publishing is a leading source for woodworking books, videos, and DVDs, but did you know that we also publish two leading magazines in the woodworking category? *Woodcarving Illustrated* and *Scroll Saw Woodworking & Crafts* are the magazines that carving and scroll saw enthusiasts turn to for premium information by today's leading artisans. **Contact us today for your free trial issue!**

WOODCARVING ILLUSTRATED

- Written BY carvers FOR carvers
- Improve your skills with premium carving patterns and step-by-step instruction for all skill levels
- Learn from today's top artists with helpful hints and new techniques for every style of carving
- New product and tool reviews
- Stay in touch with the carving community with biographies, show coverage, a calendar of events, and galleries of completed work

SCROLL SAW Woodworking & Crafts

- Written by today's leading scroll saw artists
- Dozens of attractive, shop-tested patterns and project ideas for scrollers of all skill levels
- Great full-color photos of step-by-step projects and completed work presented in a clear, easy-to-follow format
- Keep up with what's new in the scrolling community with tool reviews, artist profiles, and event coverage

To Get Your Free Trial Issue or Subscribe:
Call 800-457-9112 or Visit www.FoxChapelPublishing.com